FALKLANDS AFTERMATH:
FORCES '85

FALKLANDS AFTERMATH:
FORCES '85

Marshall Cavendish

Published by
Marshall Cavendish Books Limited
58 Old Compton Street,
London W1V 5PA

Editor	Mark Dartford
Consultant Editor	Peter Way
Art Editor	Graham Beehag
Editorial Consultant	Geoffrey Cornish
Production Controller	Richard Churchill
Picture Research	John Moore

© Marshall Cavendish Limited
MCMLXXXIV

Phototypeset by Quadraset Limited
Printed by Printers SRL, Trento and
bound by L.E.G.O., Vicenza, Italy.

CONTENTS

Logistic supply and accommodation ships in Stanley
Harbour at dusk.

INTRODUCTION

As the epic events of Spring 1982 begin to recede, the lessons from Operation Corporate have been largely digested and acted upon.

With the benefit of a little hindsight it is now possible to look back at the wider implications of that extraordinary conflict in terms of the broader role of British Forces in the world today. Additionally, an unbiased evaluation of Argentine strategy and tactics, now more accessible, help to provide an insight into how such an unwelcome incursion ever happened — and thus warn how to guard against it happening again, to ensure that the lives lost in those distant islands were not lost in vain.

Troops deploy onto a Wessex during training.

Chapter 1

FORTRESS FALKLANDS: THE GARRISON GROWS

As military and civilian building personnel continue to pour into the islands and postwar construction work gets fully under way, tensions and uncertainty continue to plague the hardy, individualistic inhabitants whose island way of life was so rudely interrupted nearly three years ago.

Servicemen on parade in Port Stanley.

I n the two and a half years since the guns fell silent on the Falklands, the Royal Engineers have made safe two and a half million pieces of potentially lethal ordnance. It has been a long-sustained exercise in courage and technical expertise whose dangers were exemplified when Major Geoffrey Ward, commander of the 'Explosive Ordnance Disposal Unit' lost a foot to an anti-personnel mine. Yet, despite the Sappers' bravery and skill at least 25,000 mines still lie buried in some 130 minefields. They are too dangerous to attempt to clear because the Argentines removed their metal tags before planting them and their plastic bodies cannot be picked up by the mine sweeping devices at present in use. They will remain where they are, according to a sapper officer, "waiting for the technology to catch up with the mines."

This means that whole areas of the Falklands will be closed off, possibly for ever, marked with skull and crossbones signs warning: 'Danger Mines'. It is a sign which typifies the perils of peace in the Falklands where before the despised 'Argies' arrived the greatest danger lay in being butted by an irate ram. Today, there are minefields everywhere, political, economic and social minefields undreamt of before April Fools' Day 1982.

Political reassurances

Politically, the islanders need constant reassurance that they will not be handed over to Argentina. Nothing would seem more categorical than Prime Minister Margaret Thatcher's broadcast to them last Christmas in which she told them: "I am not negotiating the sovereignty of the Falkland Islands with anyone. They are British. You, the people, have a right to determine your own future. That is not negotiable." This assurance was reinforced the following month by the visits of Baronness Young, Minister of State at the Foreign Office and Michael Heseltine, the Minister of Defence. Then, to make sure that the islanders fully understand the extent of the government's commitment to their right to decide for themselves, Foreign Minister Sir Geoffrey Howe told the Civil Commissioner Sir Rex Hunt during week long discussions in London in June that there was no change in Britain's refusal to discuss the Falklands' sovereignty with Argentina.

But even the evidence of the rumble of the bull-dozers as they build the £215 million airport which will make the Falklands independent of South America does not convince the 'kelpers', many of whom believe that, despite the blood and money which have been spent to keep them British, they will be handed over to the Argentines just as soon as it becomes politically feasible. They have all read the partly completed draft report on a policy for the Falkland Islands drawn up by the Commons Foreign Affairs Committee which said: "Your committee do

Defence Minister Michael Heseltine with Sir Rex Hunt at Bluff Cove in January 1984.

not believe that present policy, however necessary it may be in the short term, offers a stable future for the islands. Not only are its material and political costs burdensome, but the policy itself is reactive and inflexible and carries with it unfortunate implications for the wider conduct of foreign policy both now and in the future." The committee went on to suggest that a form of 'lease-back' was the most promising longterm solution to the dispute but acknowledged that the timetable would have to be long, probably extending over several generations. The report was blocked by Tory members of the committee but as one sheepfarmer said: "Maggie won't last for ever. I reckon we'll be Argentinian in ten years."

The villain of the piece in Falkland eyes is the Foreign Office which the kelpers believe was scheming to hand them over to Argentina before President Galtieri spoilt its plans by mounting his invasion. Now, as far as many Falklanders are concerned, only the time-table has changed.

Sir Rex Hunt, who was regarded as an amiable chap serving out his last appointment before retiring when he arrived on the islands, has become an unlikely hero for the Falklanders for the way in

Civil Commissioner Sir Rex Hunt in full ceremonial regalia during a parade in Port Stanley.

Part of the new £22 million 'Flexiport' floating dock system needed to handle the huge influx of troops and supplies.

which he has fought their cause. So, when it was suggested that he would be replaced when his tour of duty officially ended in July, indignant telexes were fired off to No 10 Downing Street. The word in Port Stanley was that the Foreign Office wanted to replace him with someone less committed to the Falklands. The Foreign Office replied by announcing that Sir Rex would stay until September 1985. But even that concession was taken as an admission that another Foreign Office plot had been snuffed out in the nick of time.

Economic ambiguities

In the face of such deep suspicion the huge amount of money being spent on the new airfield along with £22 million on a floating dock do little to defuse the political minefield. Although the benefits they will bring the islands are acknowledged they are looked upon as mainly military enterprises designed to deter the Argentines from having another go at invasion until the time is ripe for a deal to be struck. It is here that the political minefield overlaps the economic one. For, while all this money is being spent on the big projects the islanders are becoming increasingly frustrated that the economic development of the

Falklands as suggested in the Shackleton report and agreed to by the government is taking such a woefully long time. The economy of the island remains at the stage where the opening — and quick failure — of a fish and chip van is an item of major news. Mr Adrian Monk, that Falklands stalwart who retired as the island's representative in London in June, is critical of the "sluggish and ponderous attitudes" of the Overseas Development Administration.

There is a Catch 22 element in the problems of the Administration. New houses are badly needed to attract the equally badly needed immigrants to the under-populated islands. Fifty four have been built but half of them stand empty because there are not enough men to connect them to the sewage, water and electrical facilities. Adrian Monk expresses his frustration: "Either we can't get people to go out there, or they do want to go and we can't get them out. The pace of development does seem from here to be very slow."

There is, however, more to the story of the 54 'Brewster' houses than a simple inability to finish them. They have become something of a scandal. They were bought as prefabricated kits from a

Swedish manufacturer which cost £18,500 each in Britain but in the Falklands each completed house has cost some £130,000. This means that nearly half the £15 million allocated for rehabilitation has been spent on just 54 houses. The ODA said that the cost of the houses rose sharply because of problems with shipping them to the Falklands and then in delays in getting them unloaded. Six of the completed houses have been allocated to senior garrison officers and others to overseas aid staff. Their rents, ranging from £82.50 to £159.50 a month are paid by the British government. But the islanders or new immigrants will find it very difficult to afford to buy or rent the houses simply because the wages earnt by Falklanders are less than half those earnt in Britain. The tendency therefore will be for the houses — when they become ready for occupation — to be taken over by the garrison, government and senior members of the consortium building the airfield. Adrian Monk calls them "a disastrous waste of time and money", while Sir Rex Hunt is reported as saying: "The ODA pushed these houses and Brewster as contractor on us without any choice by the Falkland Islands Government. We wouldn't have had them if we had been given a say in the matter. The Swedish style was too extravagant. Something more modest would have been acceptable."

But it has been an extremely expensive lesson for very little return. Then there is the problem of the mutton. It is a tough one in every sense of the word. The Falklanders virtually exist on mutton. It is served so often it is known as '365' (the days in a year). Curiously, the islanders, though surrounded by some of the best fishing grounds in the world do not like fish overmuch. They prefer to gnaw away at their mutton in its various guises, none of which would win an entry into any known cookbook. Nevertheless it is in abundant supply and sells at only 15p a pound. Just the thing one would have thought for the lads of the Army Catering Corps to sharpen their skills on. But no, the Army imports its meat, frozen, from New Zealand and Britain at an astronomical price. At the root of the problem is the fact that the local slaughterhouse has not measured up to EEC requirements and the army is bound by EEC rules. However, in May 1984 the local butcher, Laurie Butler, signed a deal with the army whereby he will spend thousands of pounds bringing his slaughterhouse up to EEC standards and they will take 2,500 sheep a year from him, about half the garrison's requirements.

Muttonburgers succeed where fish and chips failed

In the meantime one of the islands' few new entrepreneurs, Simon Powell, is doing a roaring trade at 'Kevin's Cafe' with his muttonburgers. The cheapest costs £1.60 and the dearest, the vast 'Triple K' sets the soldiers back £3. It is, of course, the soldiers who spend the money, the locals cannot afford to. Undoubtedly, when the construction workers build up to their full strength of around 1,400, Powell, a public schoolboy, will do yet more trade.

It is these sort of enterprises that the Falklander's want. Simple enterprises which are seen to be of benefit to the community. They want more cafes, more rooms at the hotels, a wool mill, the inshore-fishery, all those things that they thought they might have by now. The point about Simon Powell's enterprise is that it is a private venture using local materials. The government enterprises simply have not materialised. There is a feeling that this is deliberate policy and that the government is committed to 'gradualism'. It also smacks of paternalism which does not go down well with the independent-minded Falklanders: "After years of neglect they now want to molly-coddle us." No islander, for example, is being employed on the airport construction work. All the men for this project are being shipped in, via South Africa, from Britain. They are being paid large amounts of money by island standards with salaries of £10,000 to £12,000 taxfree, 36 days annual leave, a termination bonus and food and accommodation provided by the company. Even so, some men have already chucked it in, complaining about the food and conditions and boredom.

What this does of course is to create two classes of people on the Falklands and some of the islanders resent the high wages the workmen are being paid. Others realise that the workmen's presence is a temporary business and tend to agree with government thinking that for them to become involved would tip their lives even further out of kilter. Nevertheless, £10,000 a year is a great deal of money for the average Falklander whose usual pay rate is £1.40 an hour. However, the arrival in Stanley of Mr David Taylor as head of the new Falklands Development Corporation promises to get things moving for the islanders. A former senior executive of Booker McConnell, a company with an enlightened overseas record, Taylor has a three year contract at £35,000 a year to accomplish twin objectives: improving the quality of life in the Falklands and bringing about their economic development. The Development Corporation will oversee the spending of much of the £31 million aid fund agreed by the British government and Taylor will have £4.6 million to spend over the next five years. He wants to see the Corporation making development loans on more advantageous terms than the local bank the Standard Chartered — which will not be well pleased as it only opened shop in December 1983 as the islands' first commercial bank — to establish local businesses such as dry cleaning and shoe repairing which, astonishingly, do not exist on the islands except as part time jobs.

Above: Controversial modular 'Brewster' houses overlooking the ever-popular Stanley racecourse.

Below: Despite considerable investment from Britain, the Falkland economy still revolves around its wool.

Wool remains Island's main industry

Nothing planned so far promises to reduce the islanders' dependence on wool and the Falkland Islands Company. They are still the weft and warp of the Falklands' economic life. The islanders see no way out of this pattern and, while they would rather not be so tied to the Falkland Islands Company most of them do not want their way of life to be changed drastically. What they would prefer would be to carry on as sheep herders but to have sufficient money as a community to pay for those things they could not afford before: proper teaching and medical facilities and the ability to pay salaries attractive enough to encourage qualified people to make their homes in the islands.

More and more they are thinking in terms not of government aid but of the bounty of the sea to provide them with the funds they need. It has already been pointed out that they prefer their tough old mutton to the delicious fish which swim in quantities round their homes, but, even more curious for an island people, they are not in tune with the sea. The people of the Orkneys and the Shetlands to whom they are so often compared have sea water in their veins. The Falklanders do not. They regard the South Atlantic as a barrier, keeping them in and for so long, keeping others out. Certainly the weather around their islands is not conducive to a close acquaintance — coping with the wind ashore poses

enough problems. But now they look out to sea and there in plain view are the fishing boats of Poland, West Germany, Italy, Japan, Spain and Russia. There are now more than 100 trawlers scooping cod, hake and bluewhiting out of the waters round the Falklands. As their traditional grounds have become exhausted by over-fishing the foreign trawlers have moved out to the virgin waters of the South Atlantic. Soon it is expected that there will be factory ships operating for the processing of millions of tons of the protein rich shrimp-like creatures called krill.

Adrian Monk views this gloomily. In a letter to *The Times* he said: "We can expect a 'Klondike' in the South Atlantic like that which in earlier times destroyed our whale, seal and penguin stocks."

Trying to create a fishing industry

What he wants is for the British Government to declare an exclusive fishing zone round the islands and charge all foreign trawlers a licence fee for fishing in Falkland waters. This suggestion is vigorously supported by the islanders who estimate that they could raise between two and three million pounds a year from such licences — and they would not have to go to sea to collect it. It was one of the commitments they expected from Baronness Young during her visit and they were disappointed when she did not make it. The most they have been able to get out of the government so far is an acknowledgement that the possibility of establishing a 200 mile fishing limit is "under active consideration at the highest level."

The Falklanders find it difficult to understand why the government is dragging its feet over what seems to be a simple exercise in sovereignty but little is simple about the Falklands, the home of simple people. The problem was put into perspective by Dr Norman A. Godman, the Labour MP for Greenock and Port Glasgow, in a letter to *The Times* in which he pointed out that the fishing grounds now being exploited by the foreign trawlers are in fact the traditional grounds of the Argentine trawlers which are now prevented from fishing them by the British navy. Those Argentinian fishing boats which have attempted to return to their traditional grounds have been turned back by the Royal Navy.

Dr Godman points out that the Shackleton report observed that the most effective way of developing the efficient management and conversation of the fisheries would be on the basis of 'friendly collaboration between Britain and Argentina' within which the fisheries could be jointly managed. He goes on to argue that "for this state of affairs to be realized the Government would have to take the initiative in advance of more formal negotiations between the two nations."

The Government would of course find it very difficult to promote such an initiative in the present state of relations with Argentina. At the same time, it is reluctant to impose a Protection Zone which would be seen by the Third World as an attempt to exclude permanently the Argentinian fishermen, some 2,000 of whom are now unemployed, from the grounds which they and their forefathers have always fished. It could also cause complications with the nations whose boats are now fishing the South Atlantic. The United Nations would ring with the accusations of old-fashioned colonialism against a government 8,000 miles away from where the fish are being caught. Truly, nothing is simple on the Falklands.

It may appear from the Falklanders' frustration with the slowness of their progress that they are becoming blasé about the efforts being made on their behalf and the large amounts of money being provided for them by the British taxpayer — the equivalent of more than £1.5 million for every member of the population of the islands. But this is not so. They remain fully aware of the debt of gratitude they owe, not only to the young men who fought and gave their lives, but also to the ordinary Briton who is paying for the island's future.

Troops and locals: uneasy truce still holds

One of the extraordinary aspects of life on the Falkland's is that the social minefield, which was the most feared of all, with some 4,500 troops heavily outnumbering the 1,890 islanders, has so far not

Not much to do for the 4,000-odd troops garrisoning the islands.

Pilots and navigators from 23 'Phandet' Squadron on standby outside their temporary accommodation look forward to getting away from it all.

erupted. Relations between the civilians and the army remain surprisingly good, despite the wear and tear of the roads, the noise of the patrolling Harriers and Phantoms and the behaviour of some of the young soldiers, bored out of their minds and full of booze, who tend to treat Stanley like any other garrison town on a Saturday night, especially when their four month tour of duty is ending. The army has also been following a policy of moving the soldiers out of Stanley in order to reduce the capacity for friction, a move which has left some of Stanley's inhabitants a little sad. They rather like having the young men about the place and they are more concerned about the possible impact of the airport workers on their way of life.

The hospital disaster

That said, it would be wrong to suggest that the presence of the army does not impose strains, often unrecognised until something goes wrong. The disastrous fire at Stanley's King Edward Memorial Hospital last April in which eight people died was just such an incident. At the Commission of inquiry into the fire, Mr George Webster, the director of Public Works gave evidence of a 'very heated' meeting on the day before the fire, between himself, Dr Alison Bleaney, the senior medical officer, and a military representative, Captain Ward. The Army was involved because the hospital treated military as well as civilian patients and Captain Ward was demanding to know why new fire hose reels had not been fully installed. Mr Webster said that he had explained that his plumbers had been withdrawn from their work on the hose reels to repair damage caused by the misuse of military vehicles. "An army vehicle tore up a water line, then an army digger dug up the water mains to Port Stanley and Royal Signallers laying a cable tore up yet another water main on two occasions."

One and a half days water supply to Stanley had been lost on one occasion and water rationing introduced because of these accidents. Mr Webster said that he told Captain Ward: "Now we have another priority, installing central heating in a government house which is to be handed over to the military."

The Commission also heard evidence that two of the fire brigade's water pump engines had refused to start. The vehicle carrying the hoses was over forty years old, and a converted Argentine fuel tanker had been the only way of getting water to the 70 year old hospital.

Dr Bleaney's evidence told the Commission about her problems in trying to get fire doors installed at the hospital. They were promised but were never ordered. She also criticised the Ministry of Defence and the Overseas Development Administration for dragging their heels over the future of the hospital, "No one," she said, "would arrive at a decision."

Dr Bleaney said she had complained that no money had been allocated for a new hospital and had also called in vain for the appointment of a hospital administrator. "There is a lack of decision making in the Falklands. I had been asking for this as far back as December 1982."

Dr Bleaney's obvious discontent carries weight because it was she who acted as the link between the Argentine commander General Menéndez and the SAS commander, Lt Col Mike Rose, when they arranged by radio to meet and talk about surrender and she was awarded an OBE for her work. But she made it clear to journalist Anthony Holden that her

Charred remains of the King Edward Memorial Hospital in Port Stanley after the fire in April 1984.

WHERE ARE THEY NOW?

Islanders — Graham and Nat Bound

"I miss the freedom most — the solitude and the quiet. Now every few hours aircraft scream overhead, and I mean scream. I'm not complaining. It's got to be. If this is the situation, if you have to defend an outpost, then you have to put up with that sort of thing. It's much better to put up with the sound of British aircraft screaming overhead than Argentine aircraft."

When Argentina invaded the Falkland Islands Nat Bound and his wife Joan were in Buenos Aires on business connected with the travel agency they ran from their Port Stanley shop. They saw at first hand the ecstatic reaction of the Argentine population to Galtieri's escapade, and do not believe that the fervid popular desire to take over the Falklands will ever diminish.

"I've never seen such hysteria. This fellow was a god in their eyes at that time. It was a dream accomplished."

The Bounds returned to an occupied Port Stanley courtesy of the Argentine military government, and nothing has been the same since.

Every year Nat and Joan Bound come over to the UK, during the European summer and the Falklands winter. It is a working holiday during which they visit their suppliers, ordering new stock in time for the Christmas season. The shop, which started off as a newsagent's some fifteen years ago, carries an amazing variety of goods. A newsagent's could not have survived, so they branched out into the gift and tourist trade, though the tourists have all disappeared since the war. There is regret in Nat's voice as he describes the changes that have taken place in their business. "The shop and its routines have changed dramatically. We are selling different things to a different clientele now. We sell to the forces and to locals, as opposed to wealthy tourists. They would come here, and they would buy and buy, and they only wanted the best. It had to be the top quality. It had to be Japanese electronics, French perfume, English clothes, and it had to be the top brand name." The shop has been forced to come down market with a bump, concentrating much more on cheap souvenirs. However, the advent of thousands of British troops has not created a new generation of Falkland millionaire shopkeepers. Concentrations of troops represent a large captive market which is monopolised by such organisations as the British NAAFI and the US PX. In the Falklands the NAAFI has outlets both in the town (off limits to islanders) and in the 'coastels', the floating living quarters installed after the war. Since

discontent did not stem solely from her problems with the hospital. She is not a born kelper. She comes from the Isle of Skye and went to the Falklands to escape from a European civilisation with which she was becoming increasingly disenchanted. Now, those aspects of 'civilisation' which she dislikes so much are arriving in the Falklands. She told Holden that she and her husband, a Falklands Islands Company manager, who arrived in the Falklands thirty years ago are 'getting out' with their two children.

The islands can ill afford to lose someone like Dr Bleaney but she would seem to be an inevitable casualty of the war and the changes it has wrought on life in the Falklands. The world outside is catching up with the kelpers. They can still disappear into the 'camp', taking care to avoid the minefields. But when they come back what do they do? Why, they watch their videos, a catalyst for change far more insidious and effective than either the Argentines or the British army.

The fire is a tragic symptom of the problems confronting a small island community faced with what is effectively a military occupation.

Penguin News — still primarily for Falklanders

In the summer of 1983 Graham Bound, owner, publisher, writer and printer of the *Penguin News*, was in England trying to find something more up to date than the ageing duplicator with which he printed the laboriously stencilled sheets of the Falklands' only local newspaper. Graham is Nat and Joan's second son. A year has passed, but the *Penguin News* is still printed in the same way, limited to a print run of 800 because that is as many as the stencils will print before they begin to break up. There is a chance that modern printing machinery may be imported to the islands by the government. If that happens, Graham is hoping to be able to use it. It would mean that he could try to change *Penguin News* from a monthly to a weekly publication. In the face of considerable odds his enthusiasm shows no sign of waning. He is hoping to get someone to come out from the UK to help him with newspaper production. The *Penguin News* occupies a large slice of his time, and he still has to make space to run his Honda motorbike agency and help in his parents' shop. One way to increase circulation would be to aim the paper more towards the forces' market, by including more of their news, sports results and so forth. But for the moment the *Penguin News* remains a local newspaper for locals, and for the expatriate the NAAFI moved in Nat's biggest selling line to the forces has been reduced to soft toy penguins.

Falklanders around the world who make up half of the readership.

Like others of his age — he is in his mid-twenties — Graham Bound finds adapting to the strange new conditions of Falklands life easier than has been possible for his parents' generation. He travels around the islands following his stories, sometimes staying away overnight if he is out in the camp, and sometimes managing to get lifts on military helicopters. He continues to work as a stringer for outside publications, filing work for the *Daily Mail*, the *Sunday Times*, and *Time* magazine. Other publications are covered by a handful of other islanders who have become part-time journalists in the last two years. Graham's advantage is that he is already covering any possible news stories for *Penguin News*. When items of international interest crop up, such as the tragic fire at the Port Stanley Hospital in 1984, the outside publications home in on him for their story.

Falklands Defence Force

In December 1983 Graham bought himself a mobile home on a small plot of land in Port Stanley. A year ago he had said, while emphasizing his commitment to the islands, that he intended to buy his own house in Stanley one day, eventually marrying and bringing up a family there. The mobile home is the first step. He has also joined the Falkland Islands Defence Force, which with around 100 members, mostly

Volunteers of the Falkland Defence Force march through Stanley. The Force has been expanded since the war.

younger men, has never been so large. They receive instruction and weapons training from military instructors.

"Graham? He'll stay on forever," says Nat Bound, adding "or as long as he possibly can. If the Argentines took over I don't think anyone would stay — maybe 1% at the most might stay on." But Nat is not so sure about his own adaptability to change any more. "It can never return to what is was. The place, the land, the islands have been wrecked beyond recognition. The thing which attracted most of the islanders, who lived and worked and stayed there all their lives was the freedom of the place. You could go wherever you wanted to, and I don't think there was such a thing as a sign saying 'Prohibited Area'. The freedom's gone from the islands, probably forever.

Minefields are everywhere. It seems that they're never going to be cleared, but at least they're identified now. Good fishing and picnic areas have gone. The youngsters can take this sort of thing in their stride, but I'm too old to change. I come over to England once a year. I like the change, but I always wanted to go back. But now I find that, really, I don't mind if I never go back again. It's wrong. It's tragic. I don't know if other people of my generation feel the same."

A major problem on the islands is the lack of civilian tradesmen such as carpenters, plumbers and electricians. Nat reiterated the need expressed by many islanders for settlers, preferably families, prepared to put up with the initial hardships and the self-sufficient lifestyle of the islands. But he also pointed out that it is difficult to encourage such immigration when no accommodation exists to house new would-be Falklanders. The fifty-four new houses, built amid considerable controversy about their high costs, have been taken over by newly appointed government staff from Britain.

Stanley war scars fade

Stanley itself is slowly recovering from the traumas of war and the intense troop activity of the first year after liberation. The military works are moving further away, particularly out towards the new airport. Forces accommodation has been moved away from the town, which has begun to lose some of its air of dilapidation. The war scars are fading, but much still remains to be done. The road through Stanley is still a quagmire, but the traffic is getting less. Partly this is due to the completion of the new 'flexi-port' facilities in March 1984, towards the east

Part-time Defence Force members fire an artillery salute on the Queen's birthday.

Nat Bound, father of *Penguin News* editor Graham, misses the sense of freedom which the war has banished forever.

end of the harbour. The new installation dwarfes the other docking facilities and jetties, and can unload large ships in record time, though it is used only by MOD vessels.

As far as Nat can see the only possible new industry which might be able to be developed sufficiently to provide much needed economic expansion is fishing. He bemoans the fact that there is no restricted fishing zone around the islands. Polish, Russian and Japanese fishing fleets, complete with factory ships, are busily scooping up the fish shoals as fast as they can in Falkland waters. The Poles use Falkland docking facilities sometimes, which is a source of revenue, but they fish very close to land. Much of the catch is sold in West Africa, showing that it is a commercial venture rather than just a state subsidized home market operation. The Russians in particular are fishing for krill, and the Bounds worry in case overfishing of this could affect the bird population which depend on it.

Along with most other Falklanders Nat Bound fears that a change of government in Britain could lead to a rapid accession to Argentine demands. As he sees it, everyone should be prepared to make concessions if any sort of an agreement is to be reached. "We have three bodies, the Argentine, Great Britain, and the Islanders. If you're going to come to any solution at all, all those three bodies must be prepared to get together and give. All three bodies are far too rigid. If they would go into it with the right spirit, I think you'd get a situation where nobody would win — but on the other hand nobody would lose."

Chapter 2

SEA WAR: THE FACTS EMERGE

Always the last to give up its mysteries, the sea lived up to its enigmatic reputation during the Falklands campaign. With increasing hindsight it has been possible to examine in more detail some of the well-known — and the less-publicised — events that took place in the chill waters of the South Atlantic.

HMS Fearless during a Mirage attack in 'bomb alley'.

To say that controversies still rage about the naval war in the South Atlantic would be an exaggeration, but it is fair to say that nearly three years later there is still a lively debate. Equally lively is the pursuit of enquiries into such questions as the sinking of the *Belgrano* and the part played by Argentine submarines and the SAS and SBS, for example.

The naval war which occurred was unique in being the first full-scale conflict at sea since 1945, and its lessons must therefore have implications for all navies. Ships have been sunk in other local wars but during the 14 weeks of fighting, two navies and their supporting air forces faced each other for the first time with a wide range of modern weapons. One of the most dangerous deductions to be drawn from the South Atlantic fighting is that it was a 'one-off affair, never to be repeated'. That war *may* never recur, but specific elements of it can and almost certainly will be repeated elsewhere, so there are lessons to be learned by everybody.

When the weaknesses of the Armada Republica Argentina are taken into account, the capture of Port Stanley on 2 April must be held up as a model of combined operations. Without doubt the Royal Marines defending were wrong-footed, but a convenient veil has been drawn over just what did happen that night. The defenders were hopelessly outnumbered and could not have held out for very long, but even the limited contingency plans went awry. Inevitably comparisons must be drawn with the remarkably effective delaying tactics at Grytviken by a much smaller force. The comparative smoothness of the first phase of Operation Rosario (Argentine code name for the invasion) contrasts with the lapse into lethargy thereafter, when thousands of troops were flown in to build up defences against a British counter-attack. The most puzzling decision was to pull out the marines, widely considered to be among the best Argentine fighting men, and to replace them by a mass of poorly trained conscripts. This left the islands totally dependent on the mainland for very large quantities of food and other vital supplies. All subsequent reports showed that the logistic support of the garrison was haphazard.

Were the Falklands to be a stepping-stone to Chile?

Chilean sources have maintained throughout that the removal of the marines provides the key to understanding the motives behind Operation Rosario. According to them it was much more than a whim of General Galtieri and the Junta to distract the mob's attention from economic problems; it was the prelude to a long-planned attack on Chile. The lack of adequate naval bases in the far south makes it impossible to use the Fleet in support of air operations against Chile, but with ships able to use

Port Stanley such operations would become feasible. There is reason to believe that Chilean intelligence reports, giving the Falklands as the objective for an assault on 1 May, 1982, followed by an attack on Chile in October 1982, were in British hands as early as January but were ignored. The logic of the Chilean argument is that the Argentine marines were moved from Port Stanley to the southern land border with Chile in preparation for the attack in the autumn. Although it may seem like hair-splitting, many people in the Royal Navy expressed doubts about the wisdom of declaring a 200-mile Total Exclusion Zone or TEZ around the islands. It created more problems than it settled, principally about the right of British ships to attack Argentine warships outside the TEZ, and led to further declarations about sinking any warship more than 12 miles off the Argentine coast. In practice it had very little effect on the movements of Argentine civilian and military ships and aircraft around the islands, and did not inhibit the Argentine Navy from initiating hostile action from well outside the 200-mile limit. In retrospect it seems nothing more than a tiresome legalistic formula intended to

The burnt-out shell of HMS *Sheffield* after the devastating Exocet attack by an Etendard of 2nd Naval Attack Sqdn.

The Thomson-CSF Agave radar. It enabled the air-delivered Exocet to lock-on to its target.

get around the fact that the British did not wish to declare war.

The creation of the TEZ lent an extra dimension to the sinking of the old cruiser *General Belgrano* on 2 May, for it enabled critics of the British Government to claim that the ship was outside the TEZ and 'innocently' heading for Ushuaia. As we have seen the British had already informed the Argentine Government that *any* warship more than 12 miles off the coast of Argentina would be treated as hostile. Nor did the Argentines show any regard for the TEZ; the carrier *Veinticinco de Mayo*'s Tracker aircraft located targets 150 miles north of Port Stanley shortly before midnight on 1 May, and a strike of eight A-4 Skyhawks was planned for first light the following morning, from outside the TEZ. Far to the south the *General Belgrano* and her escort of two Exocet-armed destroyers was maintaining a patrol line, and had been moving in and out of the TEZ. It must also be remembered that Argentina claimed a

legal right to the islands, and so for legal, political and emotional reasons, would not accept any British-imposed exclusion zone around them.

Even more conclusive is the fact that on the morning of 2 May, *before* the sinking of the *Belgrano*, two Super Etendard strike aircraft armed with one AM-39 Exocet apiece, took off for an attack on the Task Force. Only when the aircraft failed to make their rendezvous with the tanker aircraft was the mission aborted; if it had gone as planned 2ndo Escuadrilla might have sunk HMS *Sheffield* a day earlier.

The second strike by the Super Etendards of 2ndo Escuadrilla on 4 May was, as we know, a spectacular success. One of two Exocets fired crippled the destroyer *Sheffield*, causing her to be gutted by fire. The shock of seeing a modern warship reduced to a smoking hulk by a single hit was enormous, and the arguments still continue in public and private about what really happened. The Royal Navy has never made public even a summary of the Board of Enquiry, presumably for good reasons, but the result has been a spate of innuendo and criticism. What makes the whole thing even more puzzling to many is the revelation that the Exocet's warhead apparently failed to detonate.

What cannot be denied is that the photographs of the *Sheffield* after the hit revealed none of the extensive damage to upperworks and decks typical of targets hit by Exocet missiles. Unfortunately the ship's damage control organisation was unable to react fast enough to the fire which broke out in a main fuel tank, as the fire main had not been divided. Then a gas turbine-driven pump failed to start, and that, combined with a failure of the after standby diesel power generator meant that the fire-parties in the after part of the ship could not get sufficient water to fight the fire. The problem was made much worse by dense clouds of black smoke, and fire-parties found themselves unable to get through to the seat of the fire.

But all this begs the question of why the ship was taken by surprise in the first place. After all, she was equipped with the latest electronic detection equipment and rockets capable of deploying clouds of 'chaff' to decoy an incoming missile. It now appears that the electronic support measures (ESM) set may have been switched off while the satellite communications link with Northwood was in use. If that is true, it follows that the ship's fighting organisation was not expecting an air attack. Had the ESM equipment been in use it could have given a precise identification of the French radar in the Super Etendard long before the aircraft reached a firing position, and it should in theory have allowed time to fire chaff-clouds on a safe bearing. Defence would have been even more certain had the ship been armed with a close-in gun system and active jammers, but until then the Royal Navy had shown little interest in either type of equipment.

THE BELGRANO AND THE PEACE PLAN: AN ANALYSIS OF THE FACTS

More than two years after she was torpedoed by the British nuclear-powered submarine *Conqueror*, the Argentine cruiser *General Belgrano* remains at the centre of a fierce debate. With the advantage of hindsight, we can isolate the moment — 20.00 BST, 2 May 1982 — when the first of *Conqueror*'s Mk 8

torpedoes struck her amidships as the turning point in the Falklands conflict.

The sinking of the *Belgrano* concentrated everybody's minds. Of her 1,138-man crew 368 died, most of them in the devastating explosions caused by *Conqueror*'s two torpedoes. Some 25 Argentine sailors died from drowning, exposure or their wounds before the rescue operation was completed.

But *Conqueror*'s torpedoes took more than an elderly cruiser with them to the bottom of the South Atlantic. Nearly three hours after *Belgrano* rolled over and sank stern first beneath the waves, the Associated Press man in Lima, the capital of Peru, filed the following despatch to his headquarters in New York:

PRESIDENT FERNANDO BELAUNDE TERRY SAID TODAY THAT GREAT BRITAIN AND ARGENTINA WOULD TONIGHT ANNOUNCE THE END OF ALL HOSTILITIES IN THEIR DISPUTE OVER THE FALKLANDS.

THE BASIC DOCUMENT WAS DRAWN UP BY US SECRETARY OF STATE ALEXANDER HAIG AND TRANSMITTED TO THE ARGENTINE GOVERNMENT BY THE PERUVIAN PRESIDENT.

HE SAID THAT LONG AND CONTINUOUS CONTACTS BETWEEN THE TWO SIDES BEGAN YESTERDAY, CONTINUED LAST NIGHT AND EARLY THIS MORNING AND WILL BE PUBLISHED TONIGHT.

BELAUNDE SAID THAT HE WAS UNABLE TO MAKE KNOWN THE TERMS OF THE AGREEMENT IN ADVANCE EXCEPT FOR THE FIRST, ABOUT WHICH THERE IS NO DISCUSSION: IMMEDIATE CEASEFIRE.

Belaunde was unaware that, as he talked to the press, *Conqueror* had sunk the *Belgrano* and with her nearly all hope of a negotiated settlement to the Falklands dispute.

During the conflict the British government's relations with the press were under the overall control of Sir Frank Cooper, permanent under-secretary at the Ministry of Defence. Reviewing the Falklands campaign, he made the revealing comment that although his department had told no lies, it chose on occasion not to tell the whole truth. Critics of the British government have levelled the accusation that less than the whole truth has been told about the sinking of the *Belgrano*. This retreat into silence is unlikely to dispel the fog of contradictions which has hung over the affair since 4 May 1982 when the then Secretary of Defence John Nott rose to his feet in the House of Commons to answer questions two days after the sinking of the *Belgrano*. Since Nott's original statement, the government's version of events has changed so often as to cast

The *Belgrano* sinking. A World War II cruiser falls victim to torpedoes of the same vintage in a war which saw many ultra-modern new weapon systems tested for the first time in combat.
Right: The victor, HMS *Conqueror*, in company with the frigate *Penelope*.

serious doubts on the official explanation of the incident.

Countdown begins as Conqueror leaves Britain

The nuclear-powered submarine *Conqueror* set sail from her base at Faslane on 4 April 1982, two days after the invasion of the Falklands. Her mission was to police the 200-mile Total Exclusion Zone (TEZ), announced on 7 April and due to come into effect on 27 April. She was responsible not to the commander of the Task Force, Rear-Admiral Woodward, but directly to the operational headquarters of the Chiefs of Staff at Northwood, Middlesex.

On 23 April, four days after *Conqueror* had reached the waters around South Georgia, the British government issued an important rider to the imposition of the TEZ. It warned Argentina that 'any approach by Argentine warships or military aircraft

which could amount to a threat to the Task Force (our italics) would be dealt with appropriately'. This gave the British war cabinet the discretion to authorise the sinking of Argentine shipping or the downing of their aircraft both inside and *outside* the TEZ.

At about 4 pm (Argentine time) on 26 April *General Belgrano* and her two destroyer escorts, *Hipólito Bouchard* and *Piedrabuena*, put to sea from their operational base at Ushuaia in Tierra del Fuego. There are two conflicting accounts of her mission. In the first *Belgrano* and her escorts — both of which were armed with Exocet missiles — were to form the southern arm of a pincer movement on the British

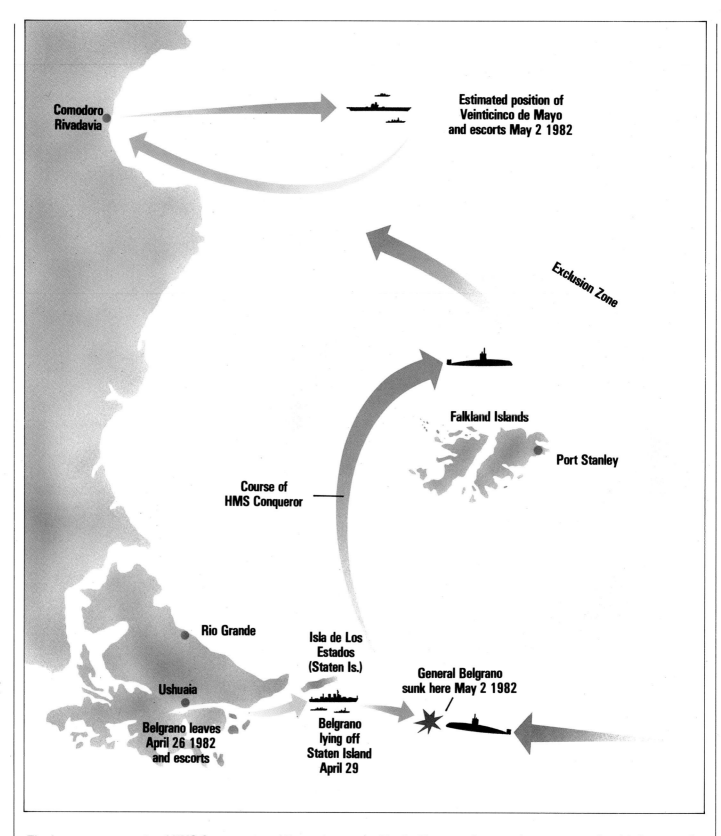

Comodoro Rivadavia

Estimated position of Veinticinco de Mayo and escorts May 2 1982

Exclusion Zone

Falkland Islands

Port Stanley

Course of HMS Conqueror

Rio Grande

Isla de Los Estados (Staten Is.)

General Belgrano sunk here May 2 1982

Ushuaia

Belgrano leaves April 26 1982 and escorts

Belgrano lying off Staten Island April 29

The known movements of HMS *Conqueror* and the major elements of the Argentine Navy's surface vessels. While much debate continues about the attack on *Belgrano*, there can be little doubt about the salutary effect it had on the rest of the Argentine fleet.

Task Force, the northern arm of which was the aircraft carrier *Veinticinco de Mayo*, her destroyer escort and a submarine, which had set sail from Commodoro Rivadavia at approximately the same time.

Belgrano's commander, Captain Hector Bonzo, has provided the second version. On 29 April, lying off

Staten Island at the toe of Tierra del Fuego, he received his sealed orders, flown in by helicopter. *Belgrano* and her destroyer escorts were to patrol a line approximately 250 miles eastward of Cape Horn, on a bearing of 110 degrees east–south-east, then back west–north-west on a bearing of 290 degrees. She was tasked to remain on the look out for any British movements either from the east or from around Cape Horn. She was not to enter the TEZ.

Diplomatic moves

News of the *Belgrano*'s sailing was passed immediately to the British by the Chileans and confirmed by American satellite. On 28 April *Conqueror* left the South Georgia area for the Falklands. On the following day there was a significant development on the diplomatic front. The US Senate debated and passed by a majority of 79 to 1 the Biden–Moynihan Resolution 382. This branded Argentina as the aggressor in the dispute and placed the United States on the side of Britain in the implementation of United Nations Resolution 502, with particular reference to the requirement for all Argentine forces to withdraw from the Falklands. On 30 April, Secretary of State Alexander Haig made a television broadcast announcing the United States' 'tilt' towards Britain after the failure of his mediation mission. He announced a number of measures to be put in hand by President Reagan, including the suspension of all military exports to Argentina and a block on new export–import bank credits and guarantees. Haig added that the President would 'respond positively to requests for material support for British forces'. Haig's statement was speedily endorsed by the President, who described Argentine behaviour as 'intransigent'. For Haig, these statements represented the culmination of the process by which he had manoeuvred the United States firmly behind Britain in the Falklands dispute.

The danger signals were immediately recognized by Peru's Foreign Minister, Javier Arias Stella, who later commented, "The moment we learned of Haig's speech, we knew that the risks of a British attack had increased immeasurably." He immediately contacted the US Ambassador to Peru, Frank Ortiz, to suggest new talks.

On the same day, 30 April, *Conqueror* reached the area which *Belgrano* had been tasked to patrol, some 120 miles east of Tierra del Fuego and 200 miles south-west of the Falklands. The sea was calm and the weather sunny. According to her captain, Commander Christopher Wreford Brown, at about 4pm on the afternoon of 30 April *Conqueror* picked up the signatures of *Belgrano*, her escorts and an oiler.

In the Falklands, the British were fulfilling Arias Stella's apprehensions. At dawn, local time, Port

Flagship of the Argentine Navy, the aircraft carrier *Veinticinco de Mayo*, main threat to the Task Force.

Stanley was shaken by the explosions of the Vulcan raid on Stanley Airport. Twenty minutes later, Sea Harriers began a further series of attacks on the Stanley and Darwin airstrips. In the afternoon the screw was tightened as naval units moved close to the shore to shell Argentine installations. British Foreign Secretary Francis Pym, who flew into Washington that day, explained that the activity was intended to 'concentrate Argentine minds'. Speaking to the press, he added that there would be no more military attacks unless any enemy ships or aircraft penetrated the TEZ. The Task Force Commander, Rear-Admiral Woodward, has offered a more precise rationale for the military activity: "My initial plan was to lay on a major demonstration of force well inside the exclusion zone to make the Argentines believe that landings were due to take place and thus provoke a reaction that would allow me to conduct a major attrition exercise before the amphibious force actually arrived."

By nightfall the Task Force had dispersed eastwards. An hour after the conclusion of Woodward's show of force, Vice-Admiral Walter Allara, aboard his flagship *Veinticinco de Mayo*, received a message from Vice-Admiral Juan Jose Lombardo, Argentine naval commander South Atlantic, ordering him to return to port with his task force, including *Belgrano* and her escorts. At 20.07 the Argentine fleet turned for home. A second message, confirming Allara's orders to all his units to withdraw, was received aboard *Veinticino de Mayo* at 01.19 on 2 May. There is little doubt that both of these messages were intercepted by the British. Throughout the conflict four Nimrod surveillance aircraft, equipped with high frequency receivers, operated from Wideawake airfield, Ascension Island. This equipment was also carried by British warships, including the carriers *Hermes* and *Invincible*. In addition the British operated a listening system from a signals station on Ascension known as 'Two Boats'. Back-up was provided by the American satellite station on Ascension — DSCS11 — which could be linked with other American–British joint satellite services to provide voice-links secure against Argentine interception and photographic surveillance of Argentine military movements.

US pro-British stance shakes Junta

At the same time as Admiral Allara ordered his fleet to turn for home, an important meeting was taking place at the Argentine Joint General Staff building in Buenos Aires. The meeting was called by General Jose Antonio Vaquero, chief of the Argentine general staff, and was attended by two members of the Junta, General Galtieri and Brigadier-General Basilio Lami Dozo. The Argentine military were shaken by the American 'tilt' towards Britain and the strength of the British response. They urged Galtieri to avoid an all-out war. Once again there is a strong possibility that this information was quickly passed to the British war cabinet by the Americans via the CIA, who had penetrated the Argentine military at all levels.

Four hours later the Peruvians came back into the picture. At 1.30am on Sunday 2 May, General Galtieri, who was still in his office at the Casa Rosada, received a telephone call from Peruvian President Belaunde. Belaunde had already had a long telephone call with Alexander Haig, in which the US Secretary of State had briefed him on the British point of view. Between them, Belaunde and Haig then thrashed out the points which were to form the basis of a renewed attempt to secure a negotiated settlement to the dispute. Belaunde put these points to Galtieri during the course of their extended discussion in the small hours of 2 May.

President Belaunde was well placed to act as a last-minute intermediary. The close ties between Peru and Argentina were a diplomatic counterbalance to the American 'tilt' towards Britain. Belaunde knew both Haig and Galtieri well and also enjoyed an excellent personal contact with the British Ambassador in Lima, Charles Wallace, whose wife he had known since childhood.

Agreement a 'single word' away

Galtieri proved responsive to Belaunde's proposals. The following morning the Argentine President handed over the detailed negotiating to his Foreign Minister Nicanor Costa Mendez. In the course of several telephone conversations, Belaunde and Costa Mendez narrowed down the Argentine

'Shuttle diplomat' Haig meets Galtieri. In the event, military actions were to overtake the political initiatives.

objections to two points. By lunchtime, from the steps of the Casa Rosada, Costa Mendez was telling reporters, 'We're on the brink of an agreement. The difference is about a single word'.

Alexander Haig had also been busy. According to his own account of the negotiations, he was 'up all night' talking to President Belaunde, who in turn was talking to General Galtieri. Communications with the British, however, were being conducted at a more leisurely pace. Although Francis Pym had arrived in Washington at 7pm on 1 May, he did not talk to Haig until the following morning at 10am. By then the British war cabinet had taken the decision to order the sinking of *Belgrano*. They did not inform Pym of the decision.

Throughout the night of 1/2 May, *Conqueror* had been following *Belgrano* along a line parallel to the TEZ. *Belgrano* was holding a steady course at about 12 knots. *Conqueror* had been following her for some 40 hours. When Admiral Lewin called at his Northwood headquarters on Sunday morning, he was informed that Commander Wreford Brown had *Belgrano* in sight. According to his own account,

Lewin then 'went straight to Chequers and called the war cabinet into a side room and told them the situation. I said we could not wait. Here was an opportunity to knock off a major unit of the Argentine fleet'. Lewin says there was then a lengthy debate. This contrasts sharply with Admiral Woodward's subsequent observations on how the decision to sink *Belgrano* was reached. In a lecture delivered in October 1982, he told his audience that approval to sink *Belgrano* was given 'in remarkably short order, reputedly in the entrance porch at Chequers'.

What remains clear is that the decision involved changing the Rules of Engagement. This presents us with another problem, for if — as the British government subsequently claimed — *Belgrano* was a threat to the Task Force within the terms embraced by the warning issued to the Argentines on 23 April, then no change in the Rules of Engagement would have been necessary. The then Defence Secretary John Nott had two bites at this particular cherry. In the House of Commons on 4 May, he said of *Belgrano* and her escorts, 'this heavily armed surface attack group . . . was close to the total exclusion zone and was closing on elements of our task force, which was only hours away.' In the same speech he presented an alternative explanation: 'Because HMS *Conqueror* might lose the *General Belgrano* as she ran over the shallow water of the Burdwood Bank, the task force commander sought and obtained a change in the Rules of Engagement to allow an attack outside the Total Exclusion Zone'. Just how big a threat did *Belgrano* represent? Her orders were not to enter the TEZ. When *Conqueror* attacked her she was steaming home and the nearest British vessel was over 200 nautical miles away — some 14 hours sailing at *Belgrano*'s top speed of 18 knots. The Burdwood Bank, frequently cited as a 'no go' area for *Conqueror*, was quite navigable. At no point was it shallower than 50 metres. The draught of a submerged *Conqueror*-type submarine is 18 metres.

A further problem remains in the unravelling of the sequence of events of Sunday 2 May. In an article published in *The Economist* in November 1983, Sir Nicholas Henderson, British ambassador in Washington during the war, stated that the decision to authorise the sinking of *Belgrano* was reached at Chequers on or around mid-day. Nevertheless, *Conqueror* did not receive the order until 14.00 local time (18.00 BST). Although *Conqueror* had been suffering from communications problems since setting sail from Faslane, Admiral Lewin has stated unequivocally — on the television programme 'Weekend World' — that 'on this occasion communications worked very quickly'. If Henderson is correct, and the decision to sink *Belgrano* was reached at mid-day, this leaves a six-hour gap before the orders came through to Commander Wreford Brown.

Conqueror had gone on to action stations at 15.00. Fifty-seven minutes later, at a range of 4,000 yards, she fired three Mk8 torpedoes. In an age of high-technology warfare, three torpedoes of a type developed in World War 2 ran on towards a cruiser which had been commissioned in 1939. There was a 43-second wait before the first torpedo struck *Belgrano* amidships sending a huge explosion blasting through four steel decks to the main deck. Seconds later, the second torpedo hit *Belgrano* 15 metres from her prow, tearing the bows away from the hull. The third torpedo missed the cruiser, ran on to strike the destroyer *Hipólito Bouchard*, but failed to explode. In *Conqueror*'s control room there were scenes of jubilation, quickly stifled when she was depth-charged by *Piedrabuena*. *Conqueror* was to spend an extremely uncomfortable couple of hours before going to periscope depth to signal news of her attack on *Belgrano*.

Belgrano sunk; talks scuttled

In Argentina, news of the sinking reached the Presidency at 18.45. Within 15 minutes it was conveyed by Admiral Anaya to the military committee which was discussing the Peruvian proposals.

The talks in Washington between Alexander Haig and Francis Pym on Sunday 2 May began at 10am — two hours after the weight of evidence suggests the decision to sink *Belgrano* was made at Chequers. They continued throughout the morning and over lunch at the British Embassy and were resumed over the telephone later in the afternoon shortly before Pym flew off to New York. What were they discussing? Two sharply contrasting pictures of the morning's diplomatic activity emerge. Both Alexander Haig and the Peruvians have stated that they were discussing the text of detailed peace proposals which Belaunde anticipated the Argentines would accept later in the day. At the press conference he called at 16.45 on the afternoon of 2 May President Belaunde said: 'The document is not a capitulation for either side. I think it has the merit of being a testament of victory . . . In a couple of hours it may be possible to advance much of the conclusion of the final text.' Interviewed in 1984 on the *Panorama* television programme, Haig told Fred Emery that after the telephone marathon, 'we were down to words, single words and specifically in two paragraphs of the . . . points, and of course these words were critical and it was critical to know whether or not they were acceptable to the British government'. When pressed by Emery as to whether in his view these points were acceptable to the British, Haig gave a cautious reply in his own inimitable fashion, 'Well, basically we arrived at some articulations that appeared they might be'. Haig has been equally cagey about the Argentines.

In an interview published in the *Observer* newspaper on 5 June 1983 he pointed out, 'There was no way of assessing the prospects of achieving an immediate Argentine consensus on the proposals. We found it difficult to know if Galtieri's acceptance would have been accepted by the Junta' — an observation prompted by the frustrations of the abortive round of shuttle diplomacy in April.

Despite Haig's calculated ambivalences, his statements — and those of Belaunde — are peppered with references to 'documents', 'texts' and 'single words'. Francis Pym has a different recollection of the talks. He has stoutly maintained that there was no detailed text discussed that morning. Had there been, 'I would have been in touch with London right away *about the words*' (our italics). In June 1984, giving evidence to the House of Commons Foreign Affairs Committee, he rejected the suggestion that all sides to the dispute had been on the brink of an agreement and described the Peruvian peace plan as 'an outline of a possible future proposal', of which there was no urgent need to inform London.

The contrast could hardly be greater. In Argentina the preceding 24 hours had seen frantic diplomatic activity, culminating with Foreign Minister Costa Mendez's announcement that 'We're on the brink of an agreement'. The Peruvians continued to push for a solution; Prime Minister Manuel Ulloa claims to have telephoned Haig, in the middle of the latter's talks with Francis Pym, to urge a one- or two-day truce between the British and the Argentines.

On the British side, Olympian detachment was the order of the day. Both Pym and Sir Nicholas Henderson have confirmed that they did not convey the Haig–Belaunde peace proposals to London until after *Belgrano* had been sunk. Nevertheless, there remains one source of information about the progress of the talks which would still have been open to Mrs Thatcher's War Cabinet — Ambassador Charles Wallace in Lima. The Peruvian Foreign Minister Arias Stella insists that 'from about mid-day that Saturday' (1 May) until well into Sunday he was in constant telephone contact with Wallace. Arias Stella has stated that he assumed Wallace was reporting back to London. Wallace, who is now British Ambassador in Uruguay, has declined to make any comment on the events of the weekend 1–2 May.

Argentines based hopes on assumptions
It is, perhaps, these Peruvian and Argentine 'assumptions' which lie at the heart of the failed initiative. The Argentines assumed that, following his statement of 30 April, Haig was in effect speaking for Britain. Thus terms that he found acceptable would be acceptable to the British. To proceed on assumptions is always dangerous, a fact underlined by Costa Mendez's account of the telephone conversation between Galtieri and Belaunde at mid-day on 2 May, in which the Argentine President confirmed Costa Mendez's agreement to the changes in the negotiating terms: 'At mid-day on 2 May, the Argentine President is in direct communication with the Peruvian President, who in turn has a direct open line to the US Secretary of State. Mr Haig, for his part, has in his office British Minister Pym, linked in turn — *it's impossible not to suppose* (our italics) — with the British Prime Minister. The circle was complete'. Clearly, however, it was not.

The British position, as we have seen, is that the War Cabinet knew nothing of the details of the Peruvian peace plan until after the sinking of *Belgrano*. According to one member of the War Cabinet, Cecil Parkinson, all that was known was a 'continuing background'. Parkinson has commented that it was against this 'background' that 'We said we must keep the military pressure up, and we must pursue negotiations and we were faced with the decision, here was a danger to our fleet and we had an opportunity to reduce the risk and we took it' (*Panorama* television interview, 1984).

Parkinson's comments underline the gulf between Britain and Argentina at this crucial point in the conflict. The Argentines — alarmed at the prospect of an all-out war for which their preparations were at best haphazard — were seeking a face-saving formula to provide them with a way out. For the British, military pressure took precedence over negotiations. In the words of Sir Nicholas Henderson, 'Even if . . . British ministers had been told that discussions had been going on between Washington, Lima and Buenos Aires . . . I do not think that they would on that account have refrained from a decision they thought necessary for the security of British forces . . . It is widely thought that if negotiations were going to lead to anything, this would only be as a result of direct and heavy military pressure'.

In effect, the Peruvian peace proposals were irrelevant to British aims. Mrs Thatcher's stern philosophy would allow nothing less than complete Argentine surrender and the restoration of British sovereignty. The *General Belgrano* was not sunk because she was an immediate threat to the Task Force, or as a cynical ploy to scupper the Belaunde peace initiative, but quite simply because she was there to be sunk. In the process, the Argentines were to be taught a military lesson in the most unequivocal terms. The lesson had a salutary effect — the Argentine fleet remained largely locked up in port for the rest of the war.

The sinking: another possible explanation, the SAS . . .
The sinking of the *Belgrano* is linked with the *Sheffield*, for it is widely believed that the Task

Force was attacked off Port Stanley. In fact nothing has been published to support this theory, and at least part of the Task Force was well to the west. What has never been admitted is how the SAS were flown into Chile, but this operation cannot have taken place before 2 May as the Task Force had not yet reached the area. Yet it is obvious that the 'stick' of SAS men and their Sea King helicopter had to come from a ship, and it is hardly likely that a comparatively slow Royal Fleet Auxiliary could have been sent ahead on such a dangerous mission. Clearly one of the carriers had to be detached, and one explanation is that the Sea King was 'staged' onto the flight deck of a civilian research ship for refuelling. If such a delicate operation was in progress to the south-west of the Falklands, the justification for sinking the *Belgrano* becomes much clearer — and the silence surrounding it.

How the French helped the British

A most remarkable feature of the air war was the skill with which the Fleet Air Arm maintainers kept the Sea Kings and Sea Harriers airworthy. Very few people expected the carrier air groups to be able to sustain intensive flying operations, but miracles occurred not once but many times over. In contrast the Argentine Navy's Super Etendards were hamstrung by a lack of spares; even though brand-new one of the five had to be 'cannibalised' to keep the other four flying. The clearest lesson in this area was the need for good logistic backup, and it must be said that there is no proof that French manufacturers supplied spares or weapons to Argentina during the war. In fact the opposite occurred, and the Argentine Government was dismayed to find that no spares could be obtained from France. Despite the repeated claims made by the British media the French Government went out of its way to supply the Fleet Air Arm, the RAF and the Army Air Corps with vital spares, from the outset.

It was never reported publicly that French Mirages and Super Etendards flew mock engagements with the Sea Harriers before they left for the Falklands. Even more helpful were a series of personal briefings by French pilots for their British 'oppos' at Yeovilton Naval Air Station. The only mystery which remains about this Anglo-French cooperation is why neither government took the trouble to explain in public, to silence the wild accusations in the media. The worst example of such crude jingoism was the story, which remains current, that French technicians showed the Argentine ground crews how to 'wire up' the Exocet missiles. If American intelligence sources are to be believed, their inspection of the Super Etendards did not reveal anything which remotely resembled an installation carried out by the manufacturers of the missile. It was at best a very rough-and-ready adap-

tation, done in a hurry, and in the opinion of at least one US specialist, the pilots deserved a medal for flying with such a dangerous contraption underneath. In fact subsequent reports by Argentine pilots included denunciations of the French for what they regarded as treachery in refusing to supply the previously agreed allocation of spares. It was not that Argentine ground crews were ignorant, but without the proper spares, handbooks and test equipment, modern weapons are extremely difficult to set to work.

Antelope, Ardent, and the aluminium argument

There was understandable public alarm in Britain and elsewhere when the frigates *Antelope* and *Ardent* were sunk. There was an immediate outcry about their aluminium superstructures, which had been criticised before 1982, and it is widely believed that their loss was somehow caused by aluminium. Before long vociferous critics were suggesting that the larger destroyer *Sheffield* and her sister *Coventry* were also sunk because of aluminium in their hulls. Here again speculation has run riot, and the truth is somewhat different. Suffice it to say that had any one of the three warships sunk by bombs been attacked with a similar load of bombs in the Second World War, nobody would have been surprised to hear that

Ardent burns fiercely after Argentine bomb attack in San Carlos Water. Although much of the aluminium superstructure melted, it took 17 air strikes to sink her.

Antelope, a Type 21 frigate like *Ardent*, sinks after her back was broken following a bomb explosion in her magazine killing the disposal expert defusing it.

they had been sunk. Even more relevant to the events of May 1982 is the fact that the *Ardent* and *Antelope* belonged to the *only* class of British warships with aluminium superstructures. The *Sheffield*, with an all-steel superstructure, burned for hours, and her sister *Coventry* rolled over comparatively quickly and sank even faster than the smaller *Ardent*.

There is no practicable way of protecting modern warships against direct hits from missiles such as Exocet, nor is there more than an even chance of avoiding major damage from a 1000lb bomb-hit. The best remedy is to keep the bombs and missiles away from the ships, preferably by destroying the 'platform' before it can launch its missiles. This goes for ship- and submarine-launched missiles as well as the air-launched type, but inevitably some will 'leak'

through the layers of defending aircraft and missiles. Once inside the two outer layers there should be a third layer of Close-In Weapon System (CIWS). This is only a modern version of the close-range anti-aircraft guns of the Second World War, and the British had actually developed the world's first missile for 'point' or self-defence, the Seacat. However, the Seacat belonged to the 1950s and early 1960s, and its replacement, Seawolf, was only just entering service in 1982. To make matters worse, the two classes of ships hit, Type 42 destroyers and Type 21 frigates, were too restricted in size to take Seawolf. The Type 42s had not even been given Seacat as it was hoped that their main armament, the Seadart missile, would be able to handle low-level targets should they ever get near. As we know the enemy did get near, much nearer than ever expected. Seacat proved reasonable but not really capable of handling modern high-speed targets. Only two Seawolf-armed ships were present, so comparisons were hard to make, but they gave an extremely good

Left: *Broadsword*. Above: *Brilliant*. Both Type 22 frigates, armed with Exocet and Seawolf missiles, whose launchers can be seen on the front foredecks. The missile guidance system radars are visible on the platforms over the bridge.

account of themselves. Although there were reports that Seawolf had been incorrectly programmed, its computer software was easily modified to cope with crossing targets. The only two ships armed with Seawolf were the Type 22 frigates *Broadsword* and *Brilliant*, and although both were in action, neither engaged an Exocet missile. However at the end of 1983 an Exocet was shot down by a Seawolf in trials off the Welsh coast, and this year the US Navy's Phalanx gun system also 'downed' an Exocet, so we know the threat can be contained. But in 1982 there appeared to be almost no way of stopping these missiles, and the British had reason to be thankful that the Argentines had only five air-launched missiles. It must have been even more gratifying to learn that the last missile was completely wasted; on 31 May it was fired into the smouldering hulk of the containership *Atlantic Conveyor*.

Misinformation, hearsay and rumour cloud the facts
In view of the fact that the two carriers returned to

the United Kingdom without any external damage did not stop the Argentines from repeatedly claiming that they had hit at least one of the ships with an Exocet. Some of the stories, which were repeated in Italian and French newspapers, can only be dismissed as ludicrous. How, for example, can we believe that HMS *Hermes* was towed into Galveston, Texas? The US Government might have been willing to carry out secret repairs, but how could the presence of a large British warship be concealed from the US press in a civilian port? Almost certainly the story arose because Argentine pilots mistook the smoke from the *Atlantic Conveyor* for fresh smoke from a burning carrier, and 'secret repairs' had to be invented to explain the undamaged appearance of the *Hermes*.

The biggest puzzle which remains unsolved since the Falklands War is the underwater war. Right from the start the British took the threat from submarine attack very seriously, for Argentina had two modern German-built Type 209 submarines and two elderly ex-American boats. Yet, despite heavy expenditure of weapons, including homing torpedoes, no Argentine submarine was sunk. Equally, no British ship was sunk, but this did not prevent the Argentine Navy from claiming that its submarines had penetrated the British anti-submarine screen with ease. Not surprisingly, this claim did not please the Royal Navy, for its current reputation rests on its capabilities as a specialised anti-submarine force in the NATO alliance. There are several related claims, that the carrier *Invincible* was hit by a 'dud' torpedo, and that an Argentine submarine was sunk in Falkland Sound.

The first point to settle is that only one submarine was operational. The old *Santa Fé*, was as we know, sunk at Grytviken, and to get her running her sister *Santiago del Estero* had been 'cannibalised'. To fool both the Chileans and the British, her gutted hull was towed to various ports during hostilites to give the impression of an operational boat. One of the two modern Type 209 boats, the *Salta*, had been under refit, and although rushed to completion, she proved

unable to complete her sea trials and had to return to harbour. Reports from American observers suggest that a torpedo 'hung up' in one of the torpedo-tubes and only two of her four diesel engines were working properly.

That left only one submarine, the *San Luis*, but she was not in particularly good condition either. As one of her diesels was not working she was taking a long time to charge her batteries. She had been used before the war to give intensive training to the crews of new TR1700 type submarines building in Germany, and so personnel were being rotated through her in quick succession. As a result two-thirds of her crew had joined only a month before, giving them little time to familiarise themselves with the complex systems on board. The biggest and most crucial defect, however, was in the fire control system, for the computer was malfunctioning. This should in theory have been avoided by using a manual back-up fire control system, which allows the operator to steer the SST-4 wire-guided torpedo by means of joystick control. According to Argentine sources the control panel for this back-up system had been wired incorrectly, and as a result commands were transposed. This error, according to the same sources, caused the torpedoes to run as much as 60 degrees off course, and as a result, although the *San Luis* escaped destruction, her attacks were entirely unsuccessful.

Argentine naval operations

Capitan de Corbeta Fernando Maria Azcueta, commanding officer of the *San Luis*, carried out a 34-day patrol in the war zone and during that patrol he made three attacks, each one involving the firing of one torpedo. The first was made against British escorts, either destroyers or frigates and presumably in company with a carrier, and the targets were an estimated 10,000 yards away. As it was night time Azcueta decided not to use his periscope, and worked instead on data from the passive sonar in the bow. Three minutes after firing the single SST-4 torpedo its guidance wire broke, but no attempt was made to work into another firing position, almost certainly because the British had detected the attack. At least one homing torpedo was launched, almost certainly a Mk 46 from a helicopter.

The second attack took place on the night of 10–11 May in San Carlos Water, against two ships, described as a destroyer and a frigate. Once again the guidance wire of the SST-4 broke, after a run of two-and-a-half minutes, but a fresh attack was ruled out as the range was opening too rapidly. We can place this attack with reasonable accuracy, and it took place almost certainly after the frigate HMS *Alacrity* had sunk the inter-island steamer *Islas dos Estados*.

The third attack was much harder, what Captain Azcueta reported as a submarine contact moving at 6–8 knots. A Mk 37 anti-submarine torpedo was fired, and a small explosion was heard on the same bearing as the target. The range is reported to have been only 3000 yards, but the target was difficult to classify, and the explosion was almost certainly not the Mk 37's warhead detonating. US intelligence sources among others, question whether any of these three torpedoes went anywhere near their targets; if they were not running accurately it would explain, for one thing, the snapping of the guidance wires. Another explanation for the first two failures is that the *San Luis* was firing from maximum range, at which distance a proper fire control solution had not been obtained. The underwater environment is particularly intractable, and in anything less than good conditions are very hard to obtain.

Informed sources in the Royal Navy deny that the carrier *Invincible* was hit by a torpedo, in direct contradiction to suggestions in the press of 'several' hits. If Azcueta's story is correct there cannot have been multiple hits on any ship, for each attack, widely separated in time and place, involved the use of only one torpedo. Of those the Mk 37 torpedo was scarcely suitable for an attack on a surface warship, being a short-range weapon designed to attack diving submarines.

From the British point of view the anti-submarine problem was distinctly unfavourable. First, the Royal Navy's entire anti-submarine effort is dedicated to warfare in the North Atlantic, not the South Atlantic. A sudden change to water of different temperatures and salinity poses severe problems to the sonars and their operators. To make matters worse the waters around the Falklands are comparatively shallow, the worst environment for most sonars. There are reports that homing torpedoes exploded after hitting the bottom, and at one stage frigates were forced to use their depth-charge mortars to blast some of the numerous wrecks littering the seabed around the Falklands, on the offchance that a submarine was lurking among them.

There was a persistent rumour that a submarine had been sunk in Falkland Sound, but considerable doubt was cast on this story when the victor was reported to be a frigate armed with Ikara anti-submarine missiles — no Ikara-armed ships went to the Falklands. Again, independent witnesses have seen both *Salta* and *San Luis* in Argentina since June 1982, so the story is clearly false. The basis of the story might be correct, on the other hand, for *San Luis* was attacked by the British in San Carlos water on the night of 10–11 May, as mentioned earlier.

German-built Type 209 submarine of the Argentine Navy, *Salta*. Reportedly not ready in time for the war, could she be the mystery submarine sunk in Falkland Sound?

Mystery missiles and mythical ships?

One mystery which never became public, and still remains unanswered is the identity of the ship which was apparently hit by a Sea Skua missile from HMS *Brilliant*'s Lynx helicopter on 2 May. Roughly eight hours after the sinking of the *Belgrano* a helicopter from HMS *Hermes* sighted the two armed tugs *Comodoro Somellera* and *Alferez Sobral*, some 90 miles inside the TEZ. It has previously been assumed that the two ships were looking for survivors but recently it has been suggested that they were actually on a minelaying mission. Whatever the truth of that, they fired on the Sea King, which promptly called up Lynx helicopters from nearby frigates, and these attacked with Sea Skua anti-ship missiles. The *Alferez Sobral* took a severe hit on the bridge but managed to limp back to port; the British helicopter crews saw a second flash and a large explosion, but turned away without identifying the ship hit. The Royal Navy claimed shortly after that they had sunk the *Comodoro Somellera*, a story which was disproved very graphically on 2 May the following year, when she laid a wreath over the place where the *Belgrano* sank.

The question which needs to be answered is, what did the Sea Skua hit at the end of its run? The two crewmen were adamant that there was a large explosion and flash, indicating a substantial hit. Ruling out far-fetched theories that the missile might have detonated a recently laid mine, we are left with the possibility that there was a second ship, which was not the *Comodoro Somellera*. In fact some commentators wonder if the *Somellera* was there at all.

There is another candidate: the ships of Task Group 72.2, the centre element of the Armada Republica Argentina's three-pronged attack on the Task Force. Argentine sources claim that Grupo 72.2 was made up of three ex-French *avisos* or coastal escorts. Two, the *Drummond* and *Guerrico* had been built for South Africa but not delivered because of a United Nations embargo. Argentina bought them both and then ordered a third, the *Granville*. The presence of three in Grupo 72.2 is clearly unlikely, as the *Guerrico* had been disabled and quite severely damaged during the capture of Grytviken at the beginning of April, when Royal Marines hit her with Carl Gustav anti-tank rockets. British sources have always maintained that the so-called 'centre prong' of the Argentine thrust was made up of two A69 corvettes, not three, which tends to support the belief that only *Drummond* and *Guerrico* were present on 2 May.

Could the mystery ship hit by a Sea Skua have been a corvette, and not the *Comodoro Somellera*? If so then the British scored a much more important hit than they realised, for they had blunted two of the three prongs of the Argentine attack (the third, as we

Coventry **ablaze. The black line down the funnel and sides was to help Task Force pilots distinguish her from the two similar Type 42 destroyers in the Argentine Navy.**

have already seen, had blunted itself). It is a tempting explanation for it also explains the mystery 'destroyer', which was said to be lying crippled in a southern port. The constant game of trying to locate and count ships has not so far turned up photographs of all three ships together, but it seems unlikely that a single Sea Skua missile would sink a 1200-ton corvette, however much above-water damage it might inflict. The damaged *Guerrico* was photographed shortly after the conflict, lying in

to keep certain details quiet, for the master plan of Operation Rosario was largely the brainchild of Admiral Jorge Anya. Even after the Junta had been replaced by a democratically-elected government the wish to protect what is left of the Armed Forces' reputation is very strong. The new Argentine Government of President Alfonsin would not enhance its prospects of survival if it were to probe too deeply into decision-making. Every nation needs legends to cling to, and at this time in its history Argentina needs to be able to look to its Navy and Air Force as defeated but nonetheless gallant losers in an unequal struggle.

British reputations have to be guarded just as much as Argentine. The finds of a Board of Enquiry into the loss of the *Sheffield* have not been made public, and some critics suggest that the 'Captains' Trade Union' has been successful in keeping those findings quiet. There is an understandable feeling that officers should not be blamed for losing their ships in battle, although this was not always the case. Until the Second World War all surviving commanding officers stood trial for the loss of their ships, even if it was no more than a formality. More questionable is the assumption that the Royal Navy's reputation must be safeguarded at all costs; official silence can never silence the questions, and uncorrected speculation will ruin a reputation just as effectively.

The Royal Navy prides itself on its high standards, particularly in anti-submarine warfare, and the failure to sink the *San Luis* rankled. The difficulty in such a situation is that *effectiveness* of tactics is hard to measure. The fact that no British ships were sunk by enemy submarine action should be sufficient proof, but it would have been much more satisfying to know that a submarine had been sunk. As it is, any number of claims can be made by the Argentines and there is no way of disproving them.

The sinking of HMS *Coventry* also caused some nervous foot-shuffling. She was operating a dual Seawolf/Seadart 'trap' with the frigate *Broadsword* on 25 May, and during a low-level attack by Sky-hawks sheered violently across the bows of the *Broadsword*. This sudden alteration of course blanked off the firing arc of the *Broadsword*'s forward Seawolf missile tracker, preventing her from getting a firing solution, and in the ensuing mêlée there was even a fear that a stray Seawolf round might have been fired into the after super-structure of the *Coventry*. Careful cross-checking and questioning of the survivors laid that ghost to rest, but the fact remains that the *Broadsword* was very nearly sunk as well, and the Royal Navy has chosen to draw a veil over the affair.

Perhaps those who wish to avoid a detailed post-mortem are right, but for those who continue to be puzzled by the enigmas of the Falklands War it is frustrating, to say the least.

harbour with a patch over the hole in her engine room, but the other two were nowhere in sight.

Reputation needs protecting on both sides

In conclusion, it is clear that neither side in the South Atlantic war have been entirely frank, nor do they have any intention of doing so in the future. Many of the questions discussed are inevitably based on hearsay, and by the very nature of things, cannot be anything else.

The Argentine Navy clearly did better than British propaganda wished the world to believe, even if it achieved none of its war aims. It is easy at this distance in time to understand the desire of the Navy

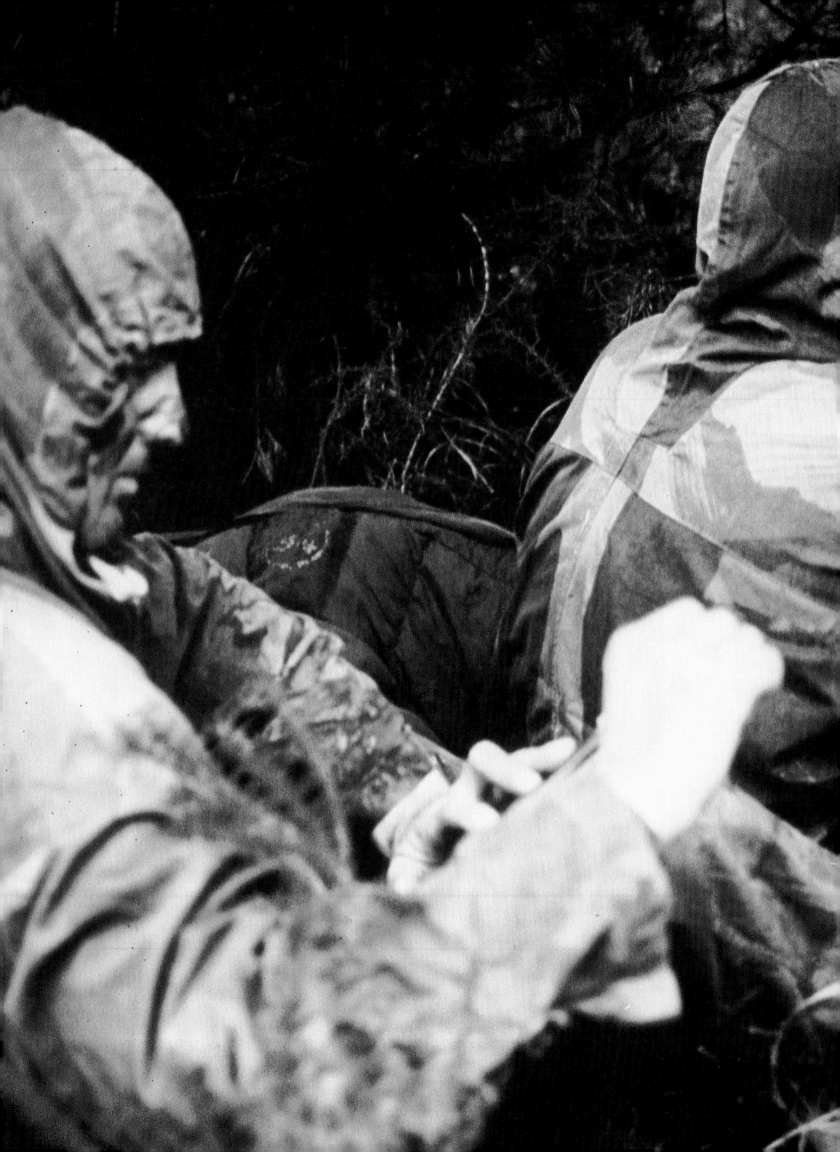

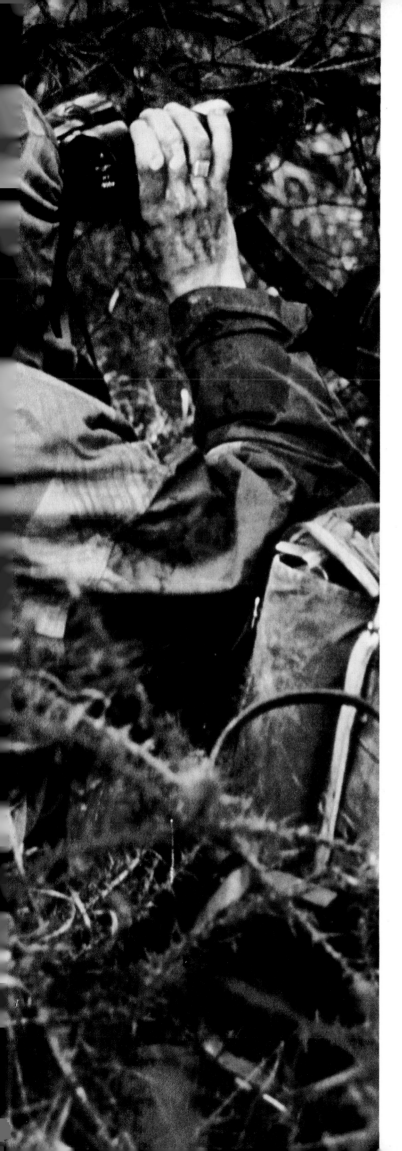

Chapter 3

LAND WAR: SPECIAL FORCES

The activities of the SAS, SBS, and other specialist units rarely come under public scrutiny. Enough is known, however, about Special Forces activity during Corporate to put together a picture of their contribution and to see how this has affected their role in the wider context of British Forces as a whole. Other countries' Special Forces make an interesting comparison with our own.

An essential part of the undercover war: SBS carry out observation ashore.

The British army has a wonderful talent for gathering together unorthodox soldiers into irregular units during wartime but the military establishment has such a horror of private armies that they are invariably disbanded once the shooting stops. They are told to get their hair cut, wear proper uniform and return to their parent regiments.

It may seem astonishing today but that was the fate in store for the Special Air Service at the end of the Second World War. The regiment clung to life under the protective mantle of the Artists' Rifles, a territorial regiment whose members, drawn originally from the unlikely ranks of artists, poets and writers, shared the unorthodox outlook of the SAS. It is because of this narrow escape from extinction that the SAS takes great pains to make people realise that it is not a 'special' unit but a regular regiment of the British Army. Similarly the Special Boat Service insists that it is an integral part of the Royal Marines and that it is properly called the Special Boat Squadron or Special Boat Section of the Royal Marines. But the antipathy among the military hierarchy towards special units has remained so strong that until this year no officer of the SAS or SBS had scaled the top slopes of the military career. It must therefore be taken as an indication of the growing acceptance of both units that two major appointments are now filled by SAS and SBS officers. Last April, Lieutenant General Michael Wilkins was made Commandant General of the Royal Marines and Major General Peter de la Cour de la Billiére was appointed Commander, British Forces in the Falklands. General Wilkins spent several years in the late 1950s in the SBS and is the first of the 'swimmer–canoeists' to achieve the marines' top appointment. Little is known about him outside the marines but Peter Billiére has already been noted as the most decorated man in the British army in 'peacetime'. He was mentioned in despatches while fighting with the SAS in Malaya, went on to win a Military Cross in Oman in 1958 and got his bar to the MC for undercover work in Aden. In 1976, in the second Omani campagin he won the DSO for exploits which were described as 'almost mythical'. Commissioned into the Durham Light Infantry he became the archetypal SAS officer, always where the action was to be found. He went on to command the 22nd SAS and then became Director of SAS. His handling of the siege of the Iranian Embassy as well as SAS operations during the Falklands War confirmed him as Britain's leading exponent of counter-insurgency tactics and brought him his latest award, the CBE. After the Falklands he spent a year at the Royal College of Defence Studies to fit himself for a top job in the army and now, as commander in the Falklands, he is filling one of the most sensitive and demanding jobs the army has to offer.

The list of battle honours on the SAS stained glass window in St Martin's, Hereford, show that the Regiment has seen almost continuous active service worldwide.

Falkland conflict gave 'respectability' to SAS, SBS as regular units

It is to the Falklands that we must look for the reason why Wilkins and Billiére have won their new appointments — quite apart from their own merit. For, while it had been recognised that the SAS is the best anti-terrorist unit in the world, the SBS was still largely unknown and neither had been able to demonstrate what they could do in the terms of modern conventional warfare. The Falklands changed all that. Their role was so vital to the success of the operation and their performance so competent and disciplined that the suspicion which surrounded them has vanished and they have become the model for the rest of the army. It is a development which is not wholly welcomed by the SAS, some of whom fear that Billiére's elevation and the acceptance of the regiment into the establishment will erode the regiment's individualism. However, despite the regiment's own reservations, the stories which are emerging about the activities of both units in the Falklands make their newly acquired status understandable.

The recapture of South Georgia, Britain's first success in the war, was largely an SAS/SBS operation. Both units were landed on the Falklands proper to establish observation posts in the heart of Argentinian-held territory. The raid on the Pucará base on Pebble Island and a number of smaller raids in which prisoners were snatched, spread alarm and despondency through the Argentinian forces. The secret operations on the Argentinian mainland frightened the junta and provided invaluable information. Finally, it was an SAS 'Psy-war' operation run by the regiment's commander, Lt Col Mike Rose, which induced General Menendez to throw in the towel.

Only one member of the SAS was killed by the Argentines during the Falklands campaign and perhaps his story will demonstate the skill, dedication and courage that the SAS and SBS took into action with them. He was Captain Gavin Hamilton, a 'new boy' who had come to command D Squadron's Mountain Troop only three months before. He was an expert climber and so was chosen to lead his troop on a reconnaissance of South Georgia. They were landed by helicopter at the third attempt and then spent a night in the open in freezing, storm force winds on the Fortuna Glacier, one of the world's most inhospitable spots. They had to ask to be lifted out the next day. Three Wessex helicopters came in to do the job. Hamilton and his men boarded one. It crashed. They got on the second. It crashed. By good fortune nobody was seriously injured. The third chopper, piloted by the intrepid Lt Commander Ian Stanley flew back to the destroyer HMS *Antrim* with his load of survivors and then returned to the glacier. His helicopter was designed to take five people but this time he crammed seventeen into it — and won a well-deserved DSO.

The following day, while the mountaineers licked their wounds, the Boat Troop made their attempt to set up observation posts. They set out in five Gemini inflatable boats, but three of them suffered immediate engine failure and had to be towed by the two serviceable boats. They were then hit by a sudden gale which parted the tow ropes. Three of the Geminis eventually got to their targets. One was found some hours later by Lt Commander Stanley who winched the three men on board to safety after they had punctured it. The other, its engine useless, was being carried by the tide swiftly down the coast. Its crew paddled desperately for land and just managed to reach shore on the southern tip of the

Some of the equipment typical in any Special Forces unit: jumpsuit, quick-release Abseil harness, handset and helmet with built-in microphone.

The RTK one-man JetRaider high speed craft designed for clandestine operations, such as close-quarter mining or observation. The constant threat of SAS and SBS was a major source of stress to the Argentines.

island. If they had drifted past there was no other land between them and the Antarctic ice. At the same time the SBS was also attempting to set up observation posts on South Georgia, with the same sort of indifferent fortune.

It was after 'inserting' an SBS team that Ian Stanley came across the Argentine submarine *Santa Fé*. He promptly attacked her with depth charges and so damaged her she was unable to dive. He called up assistance and a Wasp from the Arctic survey ship *Endurance* and a Lynx from the frigate *Brilliance* pounded the submarine with missiles and machine gun fire. She fled, leaking oil, into the

former British Antarctic Survey station at Grytviken. As the Argentines now knew that a British force had arrived it was decided to mount an attack immediately rather than wait for the 120 men of the Royal Marines M (The Mighty Munch) Company who were still 200 miles away on the frigate HMS *Plymouth*. The attack force consisted of the two SAS troops plus their headquarters unit, the SBS teams, about twenty other Royal Marines and Captain Christopher Brown of the Royal Artillery acting as spotter for the naval guns.

It was this force of some 75 men which retook Grytviken and it was Hamilton's troop which accepted the surrender of the Argentines who filed out of Discovery House without firing a shot. The following day he boarded the Wessex yet again for Leith where Captain Alfredo Astiz, the notorious torturer, had threatened to fight to the last man. But,

A typical SAS two-man team in their element: nasty weather, which in the Falklands winter was plentiful. Note the variety of non-standard equipment — British issue SLR and US M16 rifles.

faced with two troops of SAS and the guns of *Plymouth* and *Endurance*, he meekly surrendered. Hamilton then took part in the intensive patrolling of the Falklands in the search for the best landing place for the main body of the British forces. These were arduous, dangerous missions with four man sticks being landed by helicopter, sometimes twenty miles away from their objective. Getting to their posts involved night marches loaded with equipment over difficult terrain in rough weather.

It was what they had trained for on the Brecon Beacons, training which sometimes resulted in death and raised an outcry — but without which they would never have survived. They laid up during the day, scraping individual pits, covering themselves with hessian and putting turves on top of the hessian. Some SBS men became so expert at this form of horticultural camouflage that they became known as the 'Interflora Squad'. When they set out after dusk, every trace of their presence was removed. Then, when they arrived at the spot where they were to set up their observation post, they settled down for a stay (which in one case lasted 26 days) in the most extreme conditions. They could not dig their scrapes too deep or they would fill with water. They could hardly talk for fear of being heard, so close were they to the enemy's positions. Food was mostly cold tack as they could not risk lighting their tiny stoves. Frostbite was a danger. So were Argentine helicopters and Pucará ground attack planes. There was also the fear that their coded Morse messages transmitted in high speed bursts could be picked up by the Argentines' direction finding equipment.

But they reached everywhere, right into the outskirts of Port Stanley and the main Argentine encampments at Darwin and Goose Green. The SBS had other specialised duties in studying beaches and foreshores for possible landing places. While all this was going on Lt Col Mike Rose had been looking for a suitable target for his men to give the Argentines a nasty surprise. He chose Pebble Island at the northern end of the Falkland Sound where there was an airfield used by the disagreeably effective Pucarás. There was a certain historical precedent for this action because the very first raids carried out by Colonel David Stirling's original SAS in the desert in the Second World War were against German airfields.

It was decided that Hamilton would attack the airfield with his Mountain troop while the Gunner Captain Christopher Brown who had also distinguished himself on South Georgia would spot for the naval guns. Using explosive charges, missiles and their automatic rifles they destroyed eleven aircraft, including eight Pucarás. Hamilton himself destroyed four Pucarás before withdrawing his men with only two of them being wounded. It was the signal that the British were back on the Falklands. The Empire had struck back and the news not only gave a great fillip to British morale, it gave a very unpleasant shock to the Argentines.

Captain Hamilton's courageous last stand

Hamilton's last operation was a lonely one as commander of a four man patrol on West Falkland. His task was to report any movements indicating that the Argentine garrison there were preparing to attack the rear of the invasion force which had landed on East Falkland and were marching on Port Stanley. Soon after dawn on 5 June he realised that he and his wireless operator were surrounded by an Argentine patrol, possibly alerted by their signals.

In the words of the citation for his Military Cross: "Although heavily outnumbered and with no reinforcements available, he gave the order to engage the enemy, telling his signaller that they should both attempt to fight their way out of the encirclement. Since the withdrawal route was completely exposed to enemy observation and fire, he initiated the firefight in order to allow his signaller to move first. After the resulting exchange of fire he was wounded in the back, and it became clear to his signaller that Capt Hamilton was only able to move with difficulty. Nevertheless, he told his signaller that he would continue to hold off the enemy while he escaped, giving covering fire." The citation said that he was killed after "a conscious decision to sacrifice himself while facing hopeless odds" and that he was "an inspiration to all who follow the SAS."

The Argentines who killed Hamilton were so impressed with his courage they went to the home of Robin Lee, manager of a nearby sheep farm and asked if he would find them a British flag. "They said a British officer had been killed and they wanted to bury him with military honours and needed the flag. We did not believe them and now we feel terrible because they were telling the truth." The Argentine commander of the patrol made an official submission to the British forces when the fighting was over recommending Hamilton for the highest military decoration. He was in fact put up for the Victoria Cross and the SAS to a man believe he deserved it. But he was awarded the lesser decoration of the Military Cross instead.

Mr Lee also reported that once it became known that British special forces were operating on West Falkland, the Argentines became 'edgy and tense'. They captured Hamilton's signaller, a sergeant, and kept him imprisoned in a four foot deep hole under the floorboards of a farmhouse. His presence, said Mr Lee, made the Argentines 'very uneasy' but when the sergeant was released, he came out of the hole laughing. The business of keeping the Argentines 'very uneasy' was part of the recognised campaign of psy-war waged by the SAS. The citation for the DSO won by Major Cedric Delves, commander of D Squadron who led the South Georgia operations and commanded at Pebble Island, says that after the establishment of the beachhead at San Carlos, he took his men 40 miles behind enemy lines to set up a position overlooking the main opposition stronghold in Port Stanley where at least 7,000 troops were known to be based.

"By a series of swift operations, skilful concealment and lightning attacks against patrols sent out to find him, he was able to secure a sufficiently firm hold on the area after ten days for the conventional forces to be brought in. This imaginative operation provided our forces with psychological and military domination over the enemy from which it never recovered. Delves was constantly under enemy fire and, according to the citation, was an inspiration to his men in their 'unique' contribution to the conflict.

What were the SAS doing on the mainland?

These citations are important because for the first time they gave official versions of the work that the SAS and SBS were doing on the Falklands and also gave a surprising amount of information about their methods. Never before has the SAS been so forthcoming. The citations also lend credence to the claims that the SAS were operating on the mainland of Argentina. Lieutenant Richard Hutchings, a Royal Marine helicopter pilot was awarded a DSC for his courage on eight operational missions; his co-pilot, Lieutenant Alan Bennett of the Royal Navy

A SAS trooper, recognisable by the winged dagger cap-badge, puts in some practice with a Carl-Gustav anti-tank weapon. This also proved effective in the Falklands when used for trench and machine-gun nest clearance.

also got a DSC for his skill and courage "despite the particularly hazardous nature of the missions in which he was involved"; and Leading Aircrewman Peter Imrie was awarded a DSM for "several missions in very hazardous circumstances." The point about these three men and their medals is that they were the crew of a Sea King helicopter of 846 Squadron which was found burnt out in Chile, close to the Argentine border. They surrendered to the Chilean authorities three days later and Hutchings tried to explain away their presence so far away from their ship: "We were on sea patrol when we experienced engine failure due to adverse weather. It was not possible to return to our ship in these conditions."

There have been stories that they were engaged in dropping SAS 'sticks' to attack the aircraft based at the Argentine airfields at Rio Gallegos and Rio Grande whose pilots were bombing the British ships. This is extremely unlikely because there would have been no way out for the attackers and the chances of success were minimal. It is much more likely that they were engaged in landing observation parties whose job was to flash warnings to the fleet of Argentine bombers taking off to attack the fleet. The medal citations to the crew speak of a number of hazardous missions but what is not known is how many of them went to the mainland. And no other information about their flight to Chile has emerged. The SAS remains silent about this operation and the Silent Service as usual is saying nothing.

There are good political reasons for the silence about the operations on the mainland. For the British government to admit that its forces had been prowling around Argentina itself would have moved the conflict up several political notches, and similarly the Argentinian government had no wish to let its people know that British soldiers were active in their country. It is possible of course that the operation was a failure and whoever the Sea King was putting down had to hurry to safety and there really is not much more to tell. But it is a story which will continue to fascinate until someone, somewhere, spills the beans.

If it was a failure it would not have been the only

one for the SAS/SBS. We have seen how the early attempts to land observation parties on South Georgia were defeated by weather and machinery, and gremlins that bedevil every operation. There were also accidental clashes between the two units which ended in tragedy. It was inevitable that with so many observation and raiding parties roaming the Falklands in the latter stages of the conflict with the islands becoming overcrowded that such clashes might take place despite the most rigorous precautions. One SBS patrol leader was shot dead when he wandered into an SAS area, and one SAS man also lost his life. The greatest loss suffered by the SAS since the end of the war in France in 1945 was caused not by men but by a bird — a sea bird with a wing span of six feet. It fouled the tail-rotor of a Sea King carrying members of D Squadron and specialists who, while not members of the SAS, worked closely with the regiment. The helicopter was doing a simple five minute ferry job from the aircraft carrier *Hermes* to the assault ship *Intrepid* from which D Squadron was going to mount a raid on Goose Green. Instead, twenty members of the regiment and their support group were drowned when the Sea King crashed into the freezing South Atlantic. Peter Billiére said later that the regiment had lost forty percent of its sergeants in the Falklands in that one appalling incident. Most of them had taken part in the South Georgia operations and the raid on Pebble Island. They included men like Squadron Sergeant Major Malcom Atkinson who had joined the SAS in 1966 and had completed twelve fully operational tours in Malaya, Borneo, Aden, Oman and Northern Ireland. Such men are hard to find.

One of the problems caused by the accident was that at least three of the men who died were signals experts and the SAS role in the Falklands depended largely on their ability to communicate. The observation teams were using back packs which could send messages, encoded on a typewriter key board, in high speed bursts lasting only a few seconds while hopping from frequency to frequency. The units in the field were also in constant touch with their headquarters back at Hereford. There is no doubt that they used some form of satellite bouncing, probably by private arrangement between the regiment and the Americans. It was by courtesy of SAS signallers that the Prime Minister first heard that the Argentines had surrendered.

Admiral Lord Lewin, then Chief of Defence Staff, recalls what happened: "We were sitting in the War Cabinet Room in the Commons, helping the Prime Minister to draft a statement she intended to make at ten o'clock. The news that the surrender had been signed came to us by a rather roundabout route. The SAS in Port Stanley had a direct radio link to their headquarters in Hereford and were providing a running commentary. Hereford relayed it on the phone to Northwood (Operational headquarters) and Northwood relayed it to us clustered round a phone in the Commons."

The SAS helped engineer the final surrender

Radio communications also played their part in the last act of the psy-war conducted by Lt Col Rose. This war had started at a low level aimed at the ordinary Argentinian soldier. The unseen but all-pervasive presence of the SAS and SBS was unnerving. The raid on Pebble Island dismayed the Argentinian conscripts and when later their friends simply disappeared while on patrol or manning observation posts, they began to crack. The psychological pressure exerted by the SAS patrols combined with the frightening effect of naval and air bombardment softened up the Argentinian army like a boxer's punches to the body. Rose, in between commanding his forces and laying in a deck chair on the command ship *Fearless* so that he was better able to shoot at the Argentine bombers trying to sink his ship, plotted the knock out punch, designed to bring about the collapse of the Argentinians without spilling too much blood. He went to work on General Mario Menendez, commander of the Argentine forces in the Falklands.

He made contact through Captain Roderick Bell of the Royal Marines, who speaks perfect Argentinian–Spanish, and Dr Alison Bleaney in Port Stanley. The islanders use short-wave radio like telephones and Capt Bell simply called Dr Bleaney up on her frequency and asked her to contact the Argentine headquarters. She talked the senior naval officer, Captain Melbourne Hussey into coming to her office. He arrived just when Bell called back. Bell explained that he wanted to discuss humanitarian issues, the safety of Stanley's civilians and the evacuation of wounded Argentine soldiers. Hussey listened but said he could make no comment on the proposals. However he did say he would report what had been said to his government. Bell and Rose were delighted. It was the first step on the road to surrender. That was 6 June.

They called back every day at ten am and as each day brought increased military pressure so they gradually shifted the emphasis of their appeals, playing on the Argentines' sense of honour, pointing out that they had fought a good fight but now the situation was hopeless and surely both sides could agree to stop the slaughter of brave men . . . there was no dishonour in such an agreement . . . and surely Britain and Argentina should be friends, not enemies . . . There was never any reply to these messages but Bell and Rose were sure that the Argentine commanders were listening. Certainly everybody else in Stanley was tuned in to the one-sided conversation. Then, on 14 June, after three civilians had been killed by British shells and it was obvious the assault on Stanley was about to be launched, Bell broadcast a final appeal: "The position of the Argentine forces is now hopeless. You are surrounded by British forces on all sides . . . We believe that a meeting should now take place on a link kept open between the two opposing forces. If you fail to respond to this message and there is unnecessary bloodshed in Port Stanley, the world will judge you accordingly."

This time they knew the Argentines had heard and understood the message because Alison Bleaney had gone to Captain Hussey's headquarters and almost dragged him to the radio. Hussey said nothing to Bell but told Dr Bleaney that he would report the message to General Menendez. At one pm he returned to the doctor's office and asked her to pass on the message that General Menendez had agreed to talk. Later that afternoon, Rose, Bell and an SAS signaller arrived in Port Stanley by helicopter. White flags were fluttering everywhere. It was virtually all over.

The special forces Falklands armoury

Psychological warfare, otherwise 'psy-ops', form an integral and important part of SAS training. And Michael Rose is an expert at this black art. He is that epitome of the SAS officer, a thinking man of action. An Oxford degree and a teaching background allied to command of the regiment during the Iranian embassy siege and the Stansted hijack siege along with careful study of the work of psychiatrists like Dr Dick Mulder, the Dutch expert on 'siege management' have made his expertise another weapon in the SAS armoury. That armoury, as used on the Falklands, was extensive. The light-weight M16 automatic rifle was the favoured individual weapon, along with 9mm Browning pistols and hunting knives.

There was a liberal allocation of General Purpose Machine Guns and of 66mm anti-tank rockets which proved useful in blasting enemy bunkers. On the more sophisticated side, some men carried the new American Stinger hand-held anti-aircraft missiles which accounted for at least one Pucará. There was also some use made of laser aiming devices, a potentially deadly piece of 'kit'. A soldier in hiding can aim it at a target he wants destroyed. The target is then 'illuminated' so that it can be identified and locked onto the rockets and 'smart' bombs carried by strike aircraft. One the pilot is satisfied that his ordinance has acquired the laser marked target he pushes the button and his weapons should score a bulls-eye every time.

Special Boat Section (SBS) men carry out practice operations against 'terrorists' holding a North Sea oil rig to ransom. It has long been considered possible that these isolated but crucial installations could provide likely targets.

There is no doubt however that the most useful weapon carried by the SAS and SBS on the Falklands was their high speed radio with its typewriter keyboard and its 'burst' transmissions. These radios carried a huge amount of information. So much, in fact, that they showed up the inadequacies of the existing system of evaluating battlefield intelligence. This has led to a reassessment of the requirements for co-ordinating, processing and interpreting quickly enough the volume of tactically detailed and updated battlefield intelligence provided over these new super-efficient radios. Such is the speed of development of radio technology that it is now possible to build frequency hopping tactical sets which will operate with thousands of frequency changes each second with high grade encripting equipment using literally billions of unique codes to be sent by way of communication satellites. So effective are they that they have led to the establishment of a new branch of military technology called C3I — Command, Control, Communications and Intelligence. The SAS, in its determination never to fight the last war, is already studying these new sets which apart from being efficient are also lighter, smaller, and, surprisingly, much cheaper than the set they used on the Falklands.

Argentine special forces wanted to attack Gibraltar

However, the Buzo Tactico played no further part in the Falkland operations after the initial invasion. They were withdrawn to the mainland to 'await redeployment'. What that meant came to light after General Menendez had surrendered when it was revealed that a party of them, all specialised frogmen, had turned up in Spain to attack Gibraltar but had been forbidden to do so on the express orders of King Juan Carlos who, however much he wants to gain possession of the Rock, had no intention of getting embroiled in the Falklands quarrel. The Buzo Tactico is not a unit like the SAS although it is sometimes called Company 601. It is a loose collection of frogmen — Buzo Tactico means Tactical Divers — who are usually scattered in sticks throughout the marines. They only come together for special operations. However, over the years they have developed from being simply frogmen with the necessary knowledge of explosives to carry out raids and anti-shipping missions. They have also acquired skills in free-fall parachuting and undergo the intensive selection and training required of all special units. A number of them have also been trained by the SAS or SBS and have passed on that training to their colleagues. Despite that connection the Buzos remain marines while the Argentinian unit more like the SAS is the Army Commando unit which never went to the Falklands at all. Specialising in anti-terrorist operations on the mainland, it was kept back in case of trouble at home.

SAS and SBS to re-evaluate their inflatables

After their uncomfortable time with their inflatables at South Georgia they are also looking at a new type of submersible boat called the Subskimmer. It has a glass fibre hull with inflatable sidewalls which can be deflated by the pump which supplies its two-man crew with oxygen. Its powerful outboard is stopped and once it sinks under water two battery-powered electric motors take over. It has a submerged range of six miles. On the surface its outboard pushes it along at 30 knots and it can carry four divers 100 miles before the fuel in its flexible tanks runs out.

During the Falklands campaign one SBS officer insisted that the only secret weapons his men possessed were "Marks and Spencer polo neck sweaters to keep us warm!" Certainly the Gemini inflatables and the Rigid Raiders used by the SBS and the SAS now need to be augmented if not replaced by something capable of being used in a more stealthy fashion, and if the Subskimmers are not secret weapons, they could help enormously in carrying out secret operations.

The one secret weapon the men of both units possess is, of course, themselves. Their skill, dedication and panache makes them unique and they have yet to come up against a comparable enemy. Some of them were, in fact, disappointed that they did not clash with the Buzo Tactico, the Argentinian equivalent of the SBS. It was men from this specialist unit who had stormed ashore at Port Stanley and overwhelmed the Royal Marines defending Government House.

The Argentines later made much of the fact that the only men killed in the invasion were Argentines while the British suffered no casualties. But it was not for want of trying. One party of "Buzos" headed directly for the Royal Marine barracks at Moody Point and conducted a classical house clearance operation. This means that they went through every building with grenades and automatic fire with the intention of killing eveyone inside them. And there is no doubt that they would have done so if the Royal Marines had not evacuated the barracks in order to defend Government House.

The world's special forces play an increasingly important role in the age of guerrilla warfare

Most countries now find it necessary to have an SAS-style unit either as part of the army or, if they possess one, of their gendarmerie. These units have become necessary because in the age of the nuclear weapon, wars are being fought by surrogate forces, the forces of terrorism.

Perhaps the most renowned but least known of these units is the Sayaret Matkal of the Israeli army. It was this force which carried out the raid on Entebbe to rescue the passengers from a plane

West German GSG9 men treat a casualty prior to airlifting him out during a training exercise. They have their own support arms and don't need Army or Airforce assistance.

hijacked by a mixed force of Palestinian and German terrorists with the blessing of both Colonel Gaddafi and Idi Amin. But the Sayaret Matkal, whose name is never mentioned in Israel, being known simply as 'The Guys' are constantly in action. It was they who with the support of Mossad, the Israeli secret service, carried out the raid on Beirut in which three top PLO leaders were killed and masses of information carried away from their offices.

West Germany has the GSG9, formed after the fiasco of the massacre of the Israeli athletes at the Munich Olympics of 1972. The Germans found that they had no force able to cope with a large scale guerrilla/terrorist operation. They were faced with two problems: a suspicion of élite forces and the fragmentation of the police forces in the various states which made up the Federal Republic. They solved the problem by setting up their new force as part of the Federal Border Guard and named it the Grenzschutzgruppe 9. Having once decided to establish such a force, the Germans went to work with typical thoroughness. The group was given the very best equipment and underwent intensive training with help from the Israelis and the SAS.

Colonel Ulrich Wegener was appointed, and remains, its commander. He spelt out his philosophy: "We are no killer troop. What we need is disciplined, sober-minded men who by speed and decisive action make their weapons superfluous." Wegener demonstrated his men's capabilities at Mogadishu where they stormed a hijacked Lufthansa airliner to rescue the passengers. They were helped on that occasion by two SAS men who used the magnesium-based, cardboard-cased stun grenades developed by the SAS research section to disorientate the hijackers while the storming party swarmed in through the doors.

However it must be recognised that GSG9 remains only a para-military force. Its function is anti-terrorist and to help the police when confronted with armed criminals. It is not part of the army although there is little doubt that it could rapidly be transformed into an SAS type regiment.

The French anti-terrorist force falls somewhere in

between GSG9 and the SAS, known as GIGENE, the National Gendarmerie Intervention Group, it is part of the Gendarmerie Nationale which is actually the oldest regiment in the French army. GIGENE is small, numbering only 54 men. There are four officers and 50 NCOs and they are divided into three squads so that there is always one squad on alert throughout the day. They have all the usual special forces skills. Each man is a trained parachutist and all are skilled climbers and abseilers. "When I recruit a man I test him for everything", says Captain Prouteau who has commanded the group since its formation. Being such a small unit however, GIGENE, like GSG9, has no battlefield role. That is filled by the formidable Paras of the regular army.

Both Italy and Spain have similar units born from the need to combat terrorism. In Italy the role has been given to the Carabinieri who tend to rely more on traditional police, rather than the SAS, methods while Spain has set up a new Unit called the Special Operations Group (GEO). With its personnel drawn mainly from the security police and the Guardia Civile, GEO is once again a specialised police unit trained to fight terrorists rather than a regular unit of the army which counts anti-terrorism as just one of its functions. To look for precise equivalents to the SAS one must go to the Australian SAS, the New Zealand SAS and those survivors of the Rhodesian SAS who have taken up their career elsewhere. These units are based unambiguously on Hereford lines and live up to the parent unit's high standards — the Australians being particularly effective in Vietnam.

America's Delta Force and the missed opportunity in Iran

Then there is 'Chargin' Charlie' Beckwith of the United States Army and his Delta Force. Beckwith, battle scarred veteran of Vietnam, served with the SAS on an exchange posting, wangling his way to fight with them in Malaya — and it was an experience which changed his life. He quite literally fell in love with the regiment and determined to command a similar unit in the American army. But the American military establishment is even more opposed to 'funny' units than the British hierarchy and Charlie, a forceful man with a powerful command of soldier's language, made himself a great number of enemies before, eventually, in the face of the spread of international terrorism, the generals allowed him to establish his Delta Force at Fort Bragg in North Carolina. Beckwith based his unit's selection, training and methods on what he had been taught by the SAS. But he took its name from a unit he commanded in Vietnam, "a tough outfit composed of several hundred Indo-Chinese mercenary riflemen recruited and paid for by the Special Forces with CIA funds."

Iranian revolutionary troops amongst the wreckage at Desert One — where Operation Eagle Claw ended in tragic failure. Behind, a US Sea Stallion helicopter which carried part of the assault team remains largely intact.

It was Beckwith's misfortune that his new command's first task was to attempt the rescue of the American diplomats being held hostage in their embassy in Teheran. The story of the tragic failure of Operation Eagle Claw is well known. It had to be aborted when the helicopters on which its success depended ran into a dust storm and suffered mechanical failure. Then, having given the order to cancel the mission, Beckwith watched in horror as one of the helicopters crashed into a Hercules transport and started a fire in which eight men died. Beckwith sat down in the desert and wept. It was the end of the mission and the end of his dreams for Delta Force. It still exists, but under another commander and Charlie Beckwith has retired to set up his own security firm appropriately called Security Advisory Services — SAS.

It is through men like Charlie Beckwith — though not often so flamboyant — that the SAS spreads its

'Chargin' Charlie' Beckwith, robust creator of Delta Force, based his unit on the British SAS with which he served — and fell in love.

military message. It accepts pupils for training — like those from the Buzo Tactico — and also sends out small training teams which serve the dual purpose of training and winning friends in a number of armies and at the same time 'casing' potential trouble spots. It is a conscious effort to win the hearts and minds of soldiers belonging to areas where the regiments may one day be called on to operate. The SAS and SBS message is also spread by those men who retire from active service but are so committed to the lives they have been leading that they immediately join private security services operating in troubled parts of the world. Most of the protection of the Arab royal houses is undertaken by former SAS and SBS men and their particular talents are in demand wherever there is the whiff of danger.

In this way something like an SAS brotherhood is spreading round the world. It is a development which is viewed with alarm by those to whom their expertise smacks of military élitism. But the army itself now seems to have no doubt about SAS methods. In addition to the appointment of Generals Billiére and Wilkins to their senior posts the general training and formation of the army has swung towards the 'Specials' since the Falklands. The Parachute regiment is being given training similar to that of Gavin Hamilton's Mountain Troop, using Norway as a training ground. The Army Brigade for 'out of area' operations has been revamped and renamed 5 Airborne Brigade, restoring an airborne formation title to the army's Order of Battle for the first time in many years. The reason for this change of style, according to Defence Minister Michael Heseltine was to "significantly increase our ability to deploy a highly trained and professional force by air to meet any 'out of area' defence commitment . . ." It is significant that the Brigade is commanded by Tony Jeapes who won his MC fighting with the SAS in Oman in the same action as Peter de la Billiére won his.

It is all a tremendous compliment to the military prowess of the special forces and to the human qualities that make that prowess possible. As the SAS motto says: "Who Dares Wins".

Chapter 4
AIR WAR: THE LESSONS APPLIED

Harriers and helicopters certainly proved themselves in combat during the campaign, but careful analyses of every engagement have led to a number of modifications being made to these and other aircraft, particularly in the missile-delivery and on-board avionics systems on which the modern warplane is so dependent. These modifications are examined, along with the importance they will play in any future conflict.

A Harrier GR.3 firing non-guided SNEB rockets.

It is the simplest thing in the world to plan ahead to win the next war. Unfortunately the real world habitually fails to perform according to cosy predictions. For Britain, as for all NATO nations, the armed conflicts actually experienced have never for 40 years been those on which the planning and funding have been lavished.

Of course, one can draw too many conclusions from this. Had NATO ignored the possibility of a massive assault by the Warsaw Pact forces on the European Central Sector, such an attack would probably by now have taken place, and been successful. But in devoting all its ponderous energies to what are called 'in theatre' planning, the NATO countries have time and again been caught wrong-footed in sudden flare-ups in many parts of the globe. Thus, to dismiss the Falklands Campaign as a one-off aberration that could never happen again, is obviously shortsighted. Hopefully, in the long term, a political solution must be found to the Falklands dispute; but in the meantime NATO nations must address themselves to the truth, which is that anything might happen, anywhere.

Where the Falklands experience has done NATO, and Britain in particular, a power of good is in jolting everyone from Ministers down out of what had for years appeared to be lethargic entrenched positions. Funds have been unlocked for improvements that had been regarded as urgent from — in some cases — 1961 onwards! Having re-learned many lessons which are both fundamental and obvious — some as basic as the need to defend high-value warships against close-range aircraft and to have some kind of high-flying AEW cover over all friendly forces — the mid-1980s are a time of much argument. As the sound of gunfire recedes, especially from the minds of those who were not actually involved, one detects a wish for 'a return to normality'.

Too much normality in the 1960s and 1970s had resulted in a progressive degradation in the British forces, in both sheer numbers and firepower. Normality in the late 1980s is reported to include the spending of more than £11,000 million on Trident, and while no doubt an independent nuclear deterrent is essential, this sum would buy an awful lot of numbers and firepower that would be far more useful in the unexpected wars that are the ones likely to happen. This is especially the case with the air war.

The prevailing situation in Corporate was a series of traditional low-level air attacks by very ordinary aircraft, flown manually using the Mk1 eyeball for both navigation and weapon delivery, and using as weapons chiefly cannon and free-fall bombs. The means exist, even without AEW cover, to knock down virtually 100 per cent of such aircraft before they reach their targets.

Where claimed kills are concerned the SAM systems suffered badly in the detailed analyses of the

fighting which were made in 1982–83. This was especially the case with Rapier, where only one of the 14 claimed kills could be substantiated by the careful research of the authors of *Air War South Atlantic* (Sidgwick & Jackson), Jeffrey Ethell and Alfred Price. This has immediate relevance to almost any kind of war in which British forces might become involved, and at first sight the discrepancy seems disturbing. It has been explained that, in the heat of widespread action, it is easy to fall prey to wishful thinking and believe a hostile aircraft has crashed, when in fact it has not. What is beyond dispute is that the presence of British defence systems forced Argentine aircraft to attack at such low level that three-quarters of their 'iron bombs' had insufficient time to unwind the fuze safety system and become armed.

The number of kills actually achieved by the Rapier anti-aircraft system (left) during Corporate is still a matter of debate, though the initial calibration difficulties experienced after installation ashore can account for some inaccuracy in the early stages of deployment. Rapier relies in part on the precise working of delicate gyroscopic mechanisms which need to settle after movement, especially if that entails 8,000 miles of heavy seas. Portability is, however, an important feature of the system. An RAF Puma (below) lifts the system's 'blindfire' radar tracker.

Throughout the history of air warfare it has been commonplace for bombs to fail to explode, but there has never been a war in which the proportion was as high as 75 per cent. In the early days of the US involvement in Vietnam the proportion was around 20 per cent, but this was compounded by the fact that bombs dropped in close groups — for example, from triple racks of A-6 Intruders — tended to bang together and explode, destroying the aircraft, long before they could have become properly armed. This never happened in Corporate, though the obvious answer is that there were few TERs (triple ejector racks) and virtually every bomb was dropped singly. To get every bomb exploding on impact after a release at very low level the arming period must be brought down to dangerously brief values, running the risk of blowing the aircraft up with its own bombs. The alternative here is to rely entirely on retarded bombs, which have airbrakes or parachutes to pull them back far behind the aircraft, but when these are released from old-technology aircraft the already poor accuracy degrades still further.

In the USA a system called SAIF (standardized avionics integrated fusing) has been developed, and flown on the AFTI/F-16 research fighter. This automatically sets the fuzes for bombs in the final few thousandths of a second before release, so that the parameters are exactly correct. So far as is known this is not being bought for the British forces.

Though most air forces have large stocks of bombs, the inescapable conclusion in the longer term is that such ordnance will be judged obsolete. For attacks on ships the specialized anti-ship missile is vastly to be preferred, not least because it frees that

Above: Phantom F4 toss-bombing a target. This enables the aircraft to 'throw' the bomb at the target, so as to climb away from the blast after impact. Right: Beluga area denial weapon delivery system in action. The parachute allows the low-flying delivery aircraft to escape the blast. Bomblets carrying anti-personnel or anti-armour flechettes are scattered over the target zone.

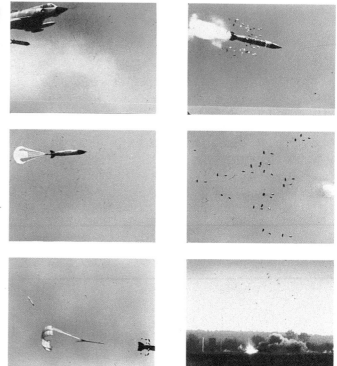

aircraft from the need to come within many miles of its target. For attacks on battlefield targets various forms of cluster dispenser are far more effective, examples being BL.755, Rockeye, MW-1 and Pégase. These greatly increase the problems faced by the defenders, whilst permitting the attacking aircraft to stay at full throttle at the lowest possible height above the ground.

Throughout Operation Corporate the main air-defence aircraft was the British Aerospace Sea Harrier FRS.1. When RAF No 1 (F) Sqn was sent south with its Harrier GR.3s it was intended these should act as attrition replacements for Sea Harriers in the defence role, but they were not needed and spent their entire war operating in the attack and reconnaissance roles. Nevertheless very important

A mixture of Harrier GR.1s, GR.3s and Sea Harriers crowd the flight deck of HMS _Hermes_ on the way to the South Atlantic. The foreground GR.3 carries Sidewinders.

modifications were made to the GR.3s which have significantly improved their all-round capability, especially in the air-defence role. Chief of these was installation of wiring for Sidewinder AAMs, which had been cleared at Boscombe in 1967 but never fitted to RAF Harriers. In the event this did not become a standard modification for all GR.3s, and even those in the war zone were soon rewired for 100 per cent attack ordnance. The point must be made that, like all manufacturers of major defence items, British Aerospace has never ceased working on studies for updating all marks of Harrier, including fitting larger wings, Lerxs (leading-edge root extensions, to enhance manoeuvrability), tip rails for Sidewinder AAMs and, not least, a proper scheme of EW (electronic warfare) installation with an improved RWR (radar warning receiver) and various ECM (electronic countermeasures) dispensers for chaff and flares and, carried internally or in a pod, an active ECM jammer.

Such studies continue to this day, but virtually nothing has got past the renewed tight-fisted control of the Treasury. There is at present little chance of

any major update in the RAF Harrier GR.3 force, as described later under the heading Ground Attack.

In contrast several things are planned to be done to the Sea Harriers. From the start of the Sea Harrier procurement process in early 1975 the financial constraints were so severe as to try to restrict the aircraft to the narrowest range of missions possible. Though primarily an air-combat fighter, it was shortsightedly thought that its only task in this role would be interception at medium to high altitudes over the open ocean of large long-range maritime patrol aircraft, such as 'Bears' and 'Badgers' which might be shadowing RN ships. Accordingly the radar was deliberately made a minimum-cost derivative of the Ferranti Seaspray helicopter set, named Blue Fox, with no look-down or shoot-down capability and virtually no effectiveness at low altitude over land. As for weapons, these were restricted to the existing Aden gun and Sidewinder AAMs.

Though Blue Fox has a useful secondary role at very low altitude in making bad-weather landings back on a ship, feeding into the pilot's HUD (head-up display) steering and height information based on the radar-derived relative positions of the aircraft and ship, it proved in Corporate to be severely limited in combat against small agile targets flying at low levels. For obvious reasons of reduced fuel consumption patrolling Sea Harriers tended to be at medium altitudes from 3,000 to 20,000ft up, and far from getting a clear radar picture of enemy aircraft many Sea Harrier pilots were either vectored towards enemy attacks by ship or land radio or acquired the targets visually. The moral was obvious: it is unwise to plan for just one type of situation, and the intention is that all Sea Harriers shall be refitted with a completely new radar of the PD (pulse/doppler) type, able to operate with clarity in the lookdown mode against the smallest and lowest targets. This new radar, for which Ferranti is prime contractor, will be a member of the Blue Falcon series. It will be partnered by something else never called for previously: a medium-ranged radar guided AAM. Sky Flash, the powerful missile in this class used by RAF interceptors, will probably not be carried by Sea Harriers, which instead will wait for the American AIM-120A (Amraam, Advanced medium-range AAM), which is smaller, lighter and is a 'fire and forget' missile which needs no assistance from the radar of the launch aircraft in illuminating the target.

All members of the original Harrier family have been rather short on pylon space. The immediate way to rectify this during the Falklands fighting was to fit twin launch shoes for Sidewinders, at a stroke doubling the number of targets that could be engaged. The Falklands war was the first occasion on which AIM-9L Sidewinders had gone into action in numbers, and they proved as big a success as the Harrier itself. The overall success rate — number of hostile aircraft destroyed divided by number of AIM-9L engagements — came out at 19/23 or 82 per cent, a figure dramatically higher than that of any previous Western AAM, and in fact much higher than most observers were prepared to predict. Against this must be set the fact that every AAM was fired from astern against a receding target attempting to escape at a high throttle setting. Had anything like a classical dogfight taken place, or had there been Sidewinder firings from other aspects, the result might have been very different. It is significant that in the very first encounter between opposing aircraft of fighter type, on 1 May 1982, Argentine Sidewinders fired from roughly head-on all failed to home on their targets.

Careful analyses were made in 1982 of the performance of both British and Argentine Sidewinders, and the general conclusion was, predictably, that the AIM-9L is a vast improvement over the -9B and other previous models. Several RAF aircraft, including the Harrier GR.3 and Nimrod MR.2, were announced as being converted to carry and fire AIM-9L, basically in a self-defence role. The total UK purchase of NATO-produced AIM-9L — made by a European manufacturing consortium led by BGT of West Germany — was significantly increased, and there is no doubt this will be the chief RAF/RN dogfight AAM throughout the remainder of the decade. What cannot be publicly discussed is what is happening to Asraam.

Asraam (Advanced short-range AAM) could have been developed with great sureness and rapidity by BAe Dynamics in the 1970s, but lack of motivation and funding caused it to be repeatedly the victim of British official indecision. Eventually the two companies were able to move ahead into a feasibility study, which in 1984 was expected to lead to engineering development lasting until 1990. Hughes Aircraft, a major US missile and radar company, joined the team in September 1982, and there is a vague intention that Asraam should eventually be adopted by, and made under licence in, the USA. An unfortunate result of the good performance of AIM-9L in combat has been to remove the pressure from Asraam and enable the development of this fundamentally newer and much more formidable AAM to proceed at a leisurely pace, with all the obvious consequences in high costs due to inflation.

Even planned increases in AIM-9L deployment are now generally regarded as unnecessary. The overwing carriage of this missile, which is standard on the Jaguar International export aircraft, has never been adopted for RAF Jaguars which continue to fly without self-defence missiles. The wingtip rails for AIM-9L featured in a 1983 BAe artist's impression of a Sea Harrier after an MLU (mid-life update) programme are not now likely to be installed. The MLU is rather imprecisely planned for 'the late 1980s', and includes the new radar and AIM-120A missile as noted previously. Fitting wingtip launchers woud increase what is called combat persistence — the number of targets a single aircraft can engage — without reducing the weapon carriage on the existing pylons, and with only modest increase in drag. No reason has been given for this apparent disinterest in a seemingly cost-effective modification, which would be of even greater value after the introduction of Asraam because this new missile is to be made compatible with existing Sidewinder launch shoes.

Of course, once the islands had been retaken it was possible to make RAF Stanley a viable airbase. After a prolonged effort clearing mines and rubbish, and extending the runway to 6,000ft (1828m), it was fitted with a pair of RHAG (runway hydraulic arrester gear) installations, as used on all RAF

Phantom bases, and from 17 October 1982 the RAF has maintained a detachment of F-4M Phantom FGR.2s at Stanley tasked in multiple roles but chiefly air defence. They carry Sky Flash, Sidewinders and SUU-23/A gun pods, and of course can carry various air/ground weapons. At first part of 29 Sqn, the aircraft were then renumbered 23 Sqn (for no obvious reason), and 15 well-used F-4J Phantoms were purchased from the US Navy at the substantial basic price of £125 million to build up a replacement squadron.

In fact this squadron will not be in the Falklands but at RAF Wattisham in Suffolk, and it will be No 74 (Tiger) Sqn which in early 1960 had been the first to equip with the Lightning F.1. For some reason the aircraft will not be known as the Phantom F.3 but as F-4J(UK), the first example in history of a British front-line aircraft not being given a mark number. A parallel case concerns the Royal Navy Sea King AEW helicopter, where the obvious mark number (AEW.6) has not been allocated more than two years after first flight. The former US Navy/Marines F-4J Phantoms have quite good commonality with the Phantom FGR.2, though the General Electric J79 engines are totally new to the RAF. Maintenance and service support will be carried out by the RAF in direct contact with the US suppliers, USAFE (USAF Europe) not being involved despite the existence of major J79 maintenance facilities supporting USAF Phantoms, some of them literally 'just down the road' from Wattisham at Alconbury.

One ought not to read too much into this purchase of secondhand and not wholly compatible aircraft. Financially poorer members of NATO, such as Turkey and Portugal, have to rely almost wholly upon combat aircraft cast off by their richer partners. Turkey's large commitment to the F-16 depends upon the nation being able to build them in an as-yet non-existent home industry. In contrast the RAF is being well supported by new replacement Harriers, Sea Kings and other types, and by the superb Tornado F.2 interceptor, which is a generation newer than any Phantom. One cannot help noting that the temporary shortfall in home-defence air strength is the immediate result of the supposed cost-saving decision to slow down the rate of production of both the versions of the Tornado, which has not only substantially increased the unit price of that aircraft — and thus the total price paid by the taxpayer for the whole force of 385 aircraft — but also delayed the entry into service of the F.2 interceptor by almost a year. The ex-US F-4J purchase is one way to give the RAF extra fighter strength at an early date, 74 Sqn being likely to get into business by about the time this appears in late 1984. The other side of the coin is that, for a very great deal of money, the RAF has got some old aircraft which the Tornado F.2 is already replacing.

Top: An F4 Phantom of 23 Sqdn (PhanDet) in the Falklands, RHAG arrester gear down. Bottom: The RAF Jaguar GR.1 does not carry air defence missiles.

As for PhanDet (Phantom Detachment) on the Falklands, this ought by spring 1985 to be in the process of moving to its splendid new runway at March Ridge, which will probably be known as RAF Mount Pleasant. At the same time No 1453 Flight, equipped with the Harrier GR.3 tasked in the close support and recon role, will probably remain at RAF Stanley, which has matured into a reasonably comfortable main base with over 1,000 personnel. The hydraulic arrester gears will be left fully operational, new installations being made at Mount Pleasant, thus providing a valuable alternate and a second runway which will still be suitable for C-130s and, in emergency, Nimrods.

Nimrod; the RAF's airborne eyes and ears

Among conventional aircraft the Nimrod is the RAF's longest-ranged armed aircraft, and with it inflight-refuelling capability — hastily added from April 1982 as it was to Vulcans and C-130s, but not to existing VC10 C.1 transports — it made eight little publicised but dramatically long reconnaissance missions during Operation Corporate to check on each occasion that there was no Argentine task force at sea. Flying a mission covering some 8,500 miles (13680km) taking most of the hours of daylight to fly along an enemy coastline punctuated by fighter bases is no easy task for an aircraft unable to defend itself against fighter attack (though Sidewinders were added later, after these missions were completed, they would hardly have deterred a Mirage). The Searchwater radar amply proved its superb qualities on each mission, and of course similar radar was fitted to Sea Kings in a 'crash programme' to produce an AEW helicopter. After the end of the fighting Nimrods flew to RAF Stanley to check out the possibilities of basing these extremely capable ocean patrol and ASW aircraft in the islands.

Two of the flights have deliberately been made non-stop from Britain, a previously unheard-of feat. The Nimrod has plenty of crew oxygen and accommodation for a relief crew, so there is really no problem. On the first end-to-end flight, not stopping at Wideawake (Ascension), in November 1983 the flight time was 18 hours 15 min. On the second non-stop mission a passenger on board was the Secretary of State for Defence, Michael Heseltine, who was brought back from his visit to the islands by a 206 Sqn aircraft to Brize Norton on 23 January 1984. Today the MR.2 fleet has been enhanced not only by Sidewinder self-defence missiles but also by adding Harpoon anti-ship cruise missiles. From the start the Nimrod has had a great capability of carrying external underwing weapons, but this was not put to use until the spring of 1982.

Of course the outstanding Nimrod AEW.3 was not cleared for service in time to provide the much-needed AEW surveillance during the fighting, and even if it had been ready it would have been very difficult to keep one in the war zone for any substantial fraction of the day because of the need for tanker support. At present the AEW.3 is entering service with No 8 Sqn at Waddington, with crew training in progress, but it is very doubtful that any will be detached to the Falklands. On the other hand up to three of the Shackletons replaced in the AEW role might be deployed to Stanley should a round-the-clock radar picket be judged worth the considerable cost.

Workhorse of the Air Bridge between Wideawake and Stanley has been the C-130 Hercules, 16 examples of which have been equipped with receiver probes and also, in the case of four aircraft, with Mk

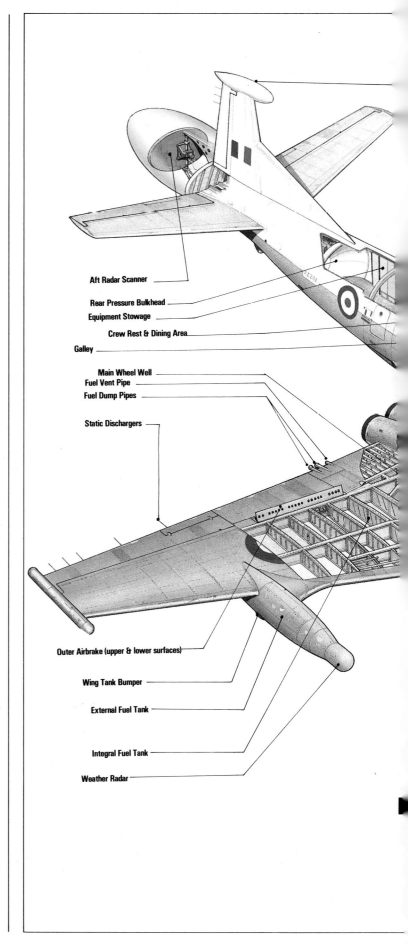

Aft Radar Scanner

Rear Pressure Bulkhead

Equipment Stowage

Crew Rest & Dining Area

Galley

Main Wheel Well

Fuel Vent Pipe

Fuel Dump Pipes

Static Dischargers

Outer Airbrake (upper & lower surfaces)

Wing Tank Bumper

External Fuel Tank

Integral Fuel Tank

Weather Radar

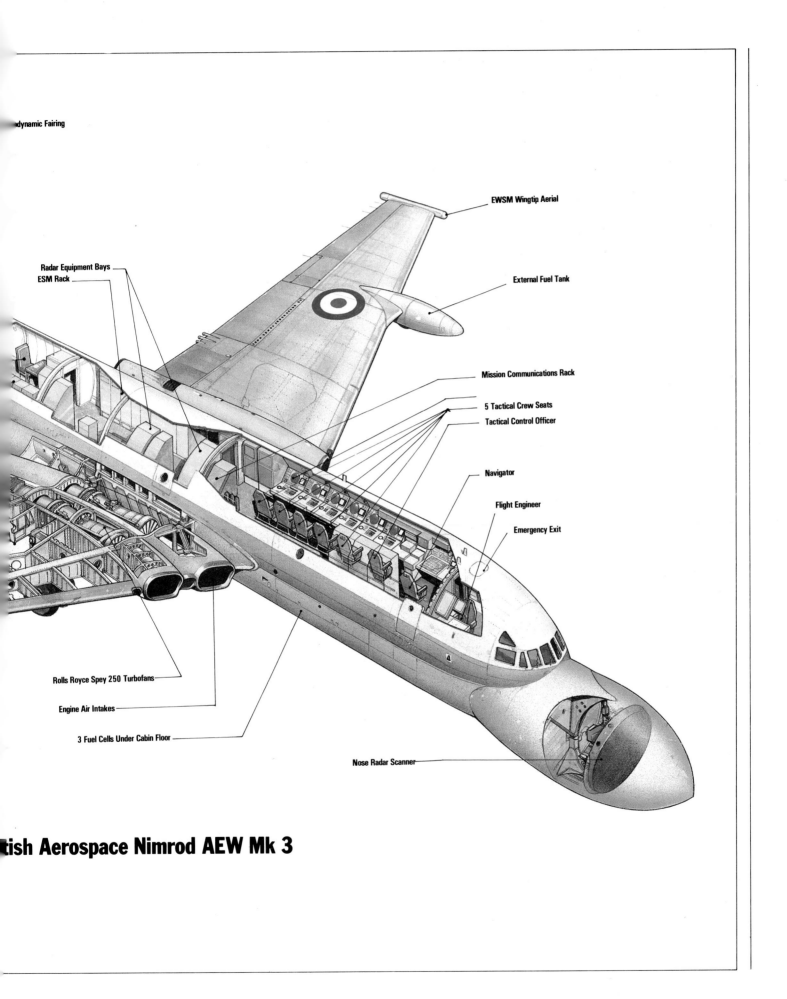

...dynamic Fairing

EWSM Wingtip Aerial

Radar Equipment Bays

ESM Rack

External Fuel Tank

Mission Communications Rack

5 Tactical Crew Seats

Tactical Control Officer

Navigator

Flight Engineer

Emergency Exit

Rolls Royce Spey 250 Turbofans

Engine Air Intakes

3 Fuel Cells Under Cabin Floor

Nose Radar Scanner

...tish Aerospace Nimrod AEW Mk 3

Above: Mk 2 ASW Nimrod with refuelling probe and armed with Sidewinder air-to-air missiles. Inset: C-130 Hercules, ubiquitous tanker/transport aircraft still the backbone of supply to the islands.
Below: View from the hose drum unit of a C-130 Hercules tanker of a Stanley-based Phantom during refuelling.

17 HDUs (hose drum units) to serve as tankers. Hercules of RAF No 1312 Flight had made 640 of these 3,360-mile (5400-km) flights by mid-1984, and the task — in early 1982 regarded as hazardous and only marginally possible — has become virtually run on an airline basis. Though severe cross-winds can be a problem no serious difficulty has been encountered operating into and out of Stanley, and with favourable winds the return trip to Wideawake can invariably be made without tanker support.

Hercules based at Stanley serve in many roles, notably as long-range search and rescue aircraft. Should any aircraft or ship get into trouble a Herc can race to the scene — compared with jets it is slow and lumbering, but it is as fast as a Spitfire — and search with its radar. Survival gear can be dropped with accuracy, and ships guided to the spot. A secondary improvement to the Hercules resulting from Corporate is the addition of close station-keeping equipment to enhance the assault para capability, and in particular to permit precision drops to be made at night.

Tristars nearly ready to shorten the air-bridge

The great distance to the Falklands from Europe, with just one intermediate airfield at Wideawake, emphasized the RAF's lack of long-range aircraft. In the 1960s, when the RAF had a global commitment, an aircraft able to carry its full load 3,000 miles (4828km) was regarded as long-ranged. Today the

improvement of high-bypass-ratio fan engines and aerodynamics of larger aircraft has resulted in the modern notion of a long-range machine being approximately doubled, to 6,000 miles (9660km). The RAF's shrinking horizons, based on disappearance of 'east of Suez' missions and almost total preoccupation with NATO, denied it any of these new-generation aircraft and thus left it ill-prepared for a sudden conflict at a distance of 8,000 miles (12900km). In the December 1982 White Paper *The Falklands Campaign: the Lessons* it was stated that wide-bodied tanker/transport aircraft were to be purchased. By good fortune British Airways was in a position to release six almost new Lockheed L-1011-500 TriStar aircraft, and these were immediately transferred to the RAF.

The Dash-500 is the latest and longest-ranged of all TriStar versions, with a shorter fuselage, long span, active flight controls and newest and most efficient RB211-524B4 engines. RAF trooping flights, painted in service colours but crewed and supported by British Airways as well as the RAF, began soon after the transfer, but once Marshall of Cambridge had built a big enough hangar the major conversion job began of turning civil airliners into either of two kinds of dedicated RAF transport. Four are Tri-Star K.1s, and the other two are K(C).1s, which instead of having passenger accommodation above the floor have cargo floors and conveyor systems so that they can carry passengers or cargo.

RAF L1011-500 TriStar being refurbished at Marshall of Cambridge. Prompted by the Falklands, the addition of these aircraft greatly enhance British forces' global role.

All six TriStars have inflight-refuelling probes, and all have a comprehensive installation of transfer fuel totalling 100,000lb (45360kg) in nine fuel cells under the floor, replacing the baggage holds. As initially converted this fuel, plus and available from the wing tankage of the basic aircraft, can be transferred through a Mk 17T HDU (hose-drum unit) in the rear fuselage. This has two quite separate drums and hose/drogue units, the main reason being to give redundancy to prevent any crisis caused by drogue damage or other unserviceability. At a future date the TriStars will be given two Mk 32 HDUs under the wings, giving them the ability to refuel three aircraft simultaneously. Operated from Brize Norton by 216 Sqn they are already totally transforming the RAF's global transport and tanker capability, and when March Ridge is able to accept aircraft — planned for April 1985 — they will make the Falklands seem much closer.

Also based at Brize are the nine recently rebuilt VC10 K.2 and K.3 tankers of 101 Sqn. So crucial is tanker strength now seen that, as the airframe lives of the Victor tankers run out, the RAF expects to convert more of its existing stock of ex-airline VC10 and Super VC10 transports, and it might well buy further secondhand TriStars or DC-10s.

For the longer term the RAF has been studying Airbus Industrie proposals for A300–600 or A310 aircraft equipped as military tanker/transports or AEW aircraft. The installations in AEW (AWACS) type aircraft are so extensive such machines have little capability in any transport or tanker role, but the obvious continuing need for capable aircraft in all three roles makes it likely that Airbus Industrie will before long be able to go ahead on aircraft in this category for several customers. Depending on the requirement such aircraft could come close to the fuel/cargo uplift of the TriStar whilst offering similar range with only two engines and reduced fuel burn. Compared with the Nimrod AEW.3 it could fly higher and for much longer, with more than twice as much internal space.

At the other end of the scale, the Falklands war had an immediate and dramatic effect on virtually every helicopter in the RAF, RN, Marines and Army. The urgent updating of machines sent to the South Atlantic, adding armour, IR-suppressing exhausts, weapons, various ECM fits and many other devices has already been described. What was perhaps unexpected was the incredible combat performance put up by all the helicopters, and especially the Sea Kings and lone surviving Chinook which often flew at maximum weight — and often far beyond it — in appalling weather for anything from 170 to 265 hours per month. Icing was an increasing problem as winter set in, but no helicopter was lost from this cause, despite air temperatures from 0°C down to minus 10°C and (in the case of Sea Kings) almost always loading up to 21,400lb (9705kg) compared with the normal limit of 21,000lb (9525kg) or, in icing conditions, 19,500lb (8845kg)!

One of the very few combat losses was a Sea King

HC.4 whose tail rotor collided with a large bird, probably an albatross. Westland have studied palliatives, such as encircling rings or French-style *Fenestron* tail rotors mounted in the centre of the fin, but such an event appears to be so rare that modification is not called for. What is more significant is that, though Westland has received contracts for Sea King HC.4s and AS.5s that more than make up for all South Atlantic losses, the demand for Sea Kings is so great that ordinary 'trucking' missions around the islands have been contracted to a civilian company, Bristow Helicopters. This is not just another aspect of government policy on privatization, but simple commonsense. The RAF/RN Sea King HC.4 and AS.5 are very fully equipped and expensive SAR and ASW machines, which have their own military duties and in any case are no more geared to carrying passengers and cargo than a bomber would be. Bristow's 23-seat S-61N airliners are far more suitable, and they fly a regular commercial type shuttle all over the islands carrying people, mail and urgent cargoes of all kinds.

In the same way, the Lynx helicopters are so packed with ASW gear, Orange Crop ESM (and many undisclosed equipments causing other bulges along the fuselage) and, in the case of the Army Lynx, a complete eight-barrel TOW missile system that they have limited ability in the passenger role. For utility transport the Gazelles are used, with one or two crew and three passengers in the back, but this is a squeeze and even the Gazelles are burdened by many items never carried in Europe. Even more important, flying in the Falklands around the clock and throughout the year rams home the vital need for comprehensive all-weather avionics.

During the fighting the Army (656 Sqn) and Royal Marines (3Cdo Bde) Scouts and Gazelles had no electronic navaids at all, and the only aid fitted as standard to the Lynx and Sea King (apart from radar in some versions) was the Decca Tans (Tactical air nav system), linked with doppler. In post-Corporate analyses it was universally agreed that, while fitting radio altimeters was a vital lifesaving provision that greatly increased helicopter utilization, a much higher equipment standard should be aimed at across the board.

Later Sea King and Lynx helicopters are being equipped with upgraded all-weather navigation aids for bad-weather and night operations at very low levels. The EH 101, now being designed jointly by Westland and Agusta, will have the best avionic fit of any helicopter, as well as complete ice protection of engines and rotors. There are still no complete or

Bristow 23-seat S-61N helicopter diverted from North Sea oil rig support operations to act as a general purpose passenger and supply carrier in the Falklands.

The surviving CH-47 demonstrates its heavy-lift capability transporting a Wessex from a County class cruiser.

ideal solutions to the problems of salt contamination and rain/hail erosion of composite rotor blades, though the twin needs of deicing (typically by electric heater elements) and structural design to withstand ground fire of up to 20 or 23mm calibre is automatically leading to answers to the erosion problem.

Chapter 5

ARGENTINA'S WAR: A DEFEAT REVIEWED

In the aftermath of any war it must serve victor as much as vanquished to evaluate the intentions, strategy and tactics of a former opponent. With the passage of time it has been possible to build up an accurate picture of Argentine plans and deployments in the war, both to provide the historian with a balanced record, and to be better informed for the future.

Senior officers of Argentina's Army, Navy and Airforce stride with the confidence of conquerors through the streets of Port Stanley in April 1982.

Most information concerning the Anglo–Argentine war available in the English-speaking world during and immediately after the conflict concentrated on the role of the British Armed Forces. A study of the conflict from the Argentine point of view, using sources which have only recently become available, makes a useful comparison with the viewpoint from the British side.

On taking over the presidency in December 1981 General Galtieri had declared that the Argentine flag would fly once more over the 'Malvinas' before the 150th anniversary of their annexation by Great Britain, i.e. by January 1983 and an invasion of the Falklands is believed to have been part of the price extracted by Admiral Anaya, the naval member of the Junta, for naval support of Galtieri as President. Whilst remaining ostensibly obdurate at the negotiating table, British interest in the Falklands seemed to have declined from the minimal to less than zero and the British Government appeared to the Argentine Junta to be practically begging to be relieved from an anachronistic colonial encumbrance.

An Argentine Buzo Tactico (SAS trained) directs dejected members of Major Noot's RM garrison away.

Although for face-saving reasons the British Government might be expected to protest fairly stridently on a diplomatic level and there might be some token international condemnation of the seizure of the islands, this would be rapidly overcome with the assistance of the United States which was assiduously cultivating Argentina as a partner in a projected South Atlantic Alliance embracing Brazil, South Africa and some of the

Joint US-Argentine forces in a training exercise a few months before the invasion.

lesser South American countries. Military reaction from Britain was unthinkable in the context of the 1981 defence cuts which would effectively reduce the Royal Navy to a rather slender anti-submarine force with no role outside the North Atlantic and even the Royal Naval Antarctic patrol vessel *Endurance*, the sole remaining permanent British naval presence in the South Atlantic, was to be withdrawn at the end of 1982.

Cautious indications of Argentina's intention to 'repossess' the islands were given on the diplomatic grapevine from the end of 1981 onwards and were followed by judicious 'leaks' of information to the Argentine press. When the British Government failed to react to these warning signals preparations for an invasion were accelerated for a target date in July 1982.

The invasion

'Operation Rosario' was precipitated three months ahead of schedule by the incident of the Argentine scrap merchants on South Georgia.

Although claimed by Argentina, South Georgia was regarded as both too insignificant and too remote from the Agentine mainland to justify occupation as part of Operation Rosario. The British reaction to the flag raising incident prompted the Argentine Junta to extend their plans to include an invasion of South Georgia with an advanced assault

on the Falklands archipelago itself. The scrap dealers arrived in South Georgia on 19 March and following the raising of the Argentine flag, HMS *Endurance* sailed from Port Stanley for South Georgia with orders to eject them. The British Ambassador in Buenos Aires was directed to instruct the Argentines to remove the naval transport *Bahía buen Suceso* from South Georgia and this vessel duly sailed on 22 March, having disembarked some men and equipment, although it remained in the vicinity. The timing of the South Georgia incident coincided with the date of the annual joint manoeuvres between the Argentine and Uruguayan Navies so that the assembly of the invasion force went unremarked.

Although the story of the invasion is now widely known, much confusion has arisen concerning the actual naval vessels and units which took part. On 25 March, the transport *Bahía Paraíso*, with a company of Marines aboard, arrived off Leith, the capital of South Georgia. The next day the submarine *Santa Fé* left its base at Mar del Plata, with a contingent of the Buzo Táctico, the Argentine equivalent of the British Special Boat Service, aboard and sailed north-eastward, followed by the frigate *Guerrico* which sailed due east.

On 29 March, ostensibly to take part in manoeuvres with the Uruguayan Navy, Task Force 20, commanded by Admiral Gualter Allara and comprising the aircraft carrier *Veinticinco De Mayo*, the old ex-US destroyers *Seguí, Hipólito Bouchard, Piedrabuena* and *Py*, the tanker *Punta Medanos* and

the armed tug *Alférez Sobral*, sailed northward towards the River Plate estuary from the main Argentine naval base of Puerto Belgrano, subsequently altering course south-eastward to rendezvous at sea with the submarine *Santa Fé*. Simultaneously, Task Force 40, comprising the Type 42 destroyers *Hércules* and *Santísima Trinidad*, the frigates *Drummond* and *Granville*, the landing ship *Cabo San Antonio*, the transport *Isla De Los Estados* and the icebreaker *Almirante Irizar*, headed southward towards Puerto Deseado. Aboard this group were elements of the 2nd Marine Infantry Battalion, the Amphibious Vehicles Battalion, with 13 LVTP-7 tracked, amphibious armoured personnel carriers and 6 LARC-5 amphibious trucks and the Amphibious Reconnaissance Company, in all about 1,200 men under the command of Rear-Admiral Carlos Busser.

Invaders land under cover of darkness
The invasion began at 9.15pm on 1 April when the destroyer *Santísima Trinidad* anchored off Port Harriet and disembarked 77 members of the Amphibious Reconnaissance Company into inflatable boats. These landed, without opposition, at Mullett Creek at 10.30pm, rapidly securing Cape Pembroke lighthouse at the mouth of Stanley Harbour. Two companies of the 2nd Marines followed at midnight in landing craft from the *Cabo San Antonio*, fanning out to take the airport, the runways of which had been blocked by vehicles. A landing site had been chosen at a point on the south side of Stanley Harbour and at 2.00am 15 frogmen of the Buzo Tactico disembarked from the submarine *Santa Fé* at the mouth of the harbour to secure this objective.

The first LVTPs, carrying 200 men of the 25th Infantry Regiment, came ashore at 6.15am, meeting light initial resistance before rolling on to link up with the group from the *Santísima Trinidad* together with whom they converged on Government House. More or less simultaneously, 150 members of the 2nd Marines were landed from helicopters at Mullett Creek, a further force of 70, also landed by helicopter, discovering that the Royal Marine barracks at Moody Brook was untenanted. At the same time a single Sea King helicopter airlifted a platoon of the 9th Engineers from the *Almirante Irizar* to the now secure airport which was ready to receive the first Hercules transport aircraft at 8.30am or 55 minutes before Governor Hunt and the 79 man Royal Marine garrison finally surrendered. Argentine losses in the operation were one dead and two wounded and an LVTP disabled.

Meanwhile the frigate *Guerrico*, carrying two platoons of Marines and an Army Puma helicopter, had linked up with *Bahía Paraíso* off South Georgia to form Task Force 60. A reconnaissance flight by an

Above: Argentine icebreaker turned hospital ship *Almirante Irizar*. Right: Despite British attacks on the Port Stanley airstrip, reinforcements were flown in under cover of darkness.

Alouette helicopter from *Bahía Paraíso* at 11.00am on 3 April revealed no sign of the 22 Royal Marines known to be on the island and the Puma airlifted 15 marines ashore an hour later, being hit by small arms fire from the well concealed defenders and crashing with the loss of two dead and several wounded. The British also succeeded in scoring two hits on *Guerrico* with anti-tank rocket projectors before being ordered to surrender. The contemporary report of the loss of *Bahía Paraíso*'s Alouette helicopter was however erroneous.

In Buenos Aires and throughout Argentina the news of the 'reconquest of the Malvinas' was received with rapture, the crowds which days before had demonstrated against the Junta now expressing delirious support for the successful military operation.

The Occupation — speak Spanish and drive on the right
A massive airlift of personnel and equipment was now mounted, a total of 9,000 personnel and 5,000 tons of equipment being flown in during the month of April and subsequently redeployed within the islands by helicopter and naval transport. During the first two weeks of April additional supplies were brought in by sea although the sea-lift diminished once the British-declared Total Exclusion Zone came into effect on 12 April. After the surrender of the British garrison, the remainder of the 25th Infantry Regiment and the 9th Engineer Company were

Above: Heady days of victory for the first troops onto the islands. Left: Admiral Busser and colleagues, behind them an Argentine flag and a British police notice are uneasy companions at the entrance to Stanley's church.

with 13 at Stanley and half-a-dozen each at Goose Green and Pebble Island. The Air Force also brought in two Chinook and two Bell 212 helicopters, the latter being used for air-sea rescue at Stanley.

Occupiers snubbed by Islanders

British accounts have naturally concentrated on the negative aspects of the Argentine occupation such as the edict issued by the Argentine military commander on the first day of the occupation with regard to the use of the Spanish language, the metric system and driving on the right. Generally the behaviour of the occupiers was correct at first although most attempts at cordiality were rebuffed by the islanders. Of considerable interest in the context of the years of neglect of the islands by Britain was the Communique issued by the Argentine Junta on 5 April which stated that measures would be taken to ensure the provision of public services and the administration of justice and

flown in from the mainland, followed by the 8th Infantry Regiment and the IXth Brigade command. The entire IIIrd and Xth Infantry Brigades were also subsequently flown in, their heavy equipment following by sea.

The airstrips at Pebble Island and Goose Green were occupied, by the Navy and Air Force respectively, 25 Pucará ground attack aircraft of the Air Force's II and III Attack and Reconnaissance Squadrons being redeployed from their normal bases guaranteed all the rights of the inhabitants. It also undertook to bring about an improvement in the living standards of the population through preserving and expanding jobs, improving the supply system from the mainland, providing banks, a permanent postal service, television and radio and better medical services and announced that every effort would be made to respect and preserve the lifestyle of the population.

The commitment regarding the provision of a television service was given top priority in the light of the approaching World Cup, powerful reception antennae and boosters being installed and television sets offered to the inhabitants at heavily subsidized hire purchase rates. Ironically, the British reinvasion of the islands took place before the second installment fell due so that now most of the Kelpers enjoy an almost free television service — courtesy of the Argentine Government!

Preparing for the worst as the Task Force sets sail

Although the invasion of the Falklands had been carried out in the belief that Britain would not react on a military level, it rapidly became apparent that, even with the reduced means at its disposal, the British Government was fully prepared to do so. Although Argentine hopes still reposed in the ability of the United States to produce a mutually acceptable diplomatic solution, positive moves were made to optimize the defensive means at Argentina's disposal.

The garrison of the islands, comprising the major elements of three of the Argentine Army's twelve brigades, was judged to have reached the maximum level which could be effectively supplied by airlift in the presence of the British sea blockade and the continuing tension with Chile over the Beagle Channel also demanded that the elite mountain brigades stationed along the Argentine–Chilean frontier should be left intact and in position. As the Falkland terrain consisted of a mixture of peat bog and mountain, no heavy armoured vehicles were transferred to the islands.

Almost all of the major elements of the Navy were standing by to provide the maximum possible resistance to the Task Force which Britain was already preparing for the counter-invasion of the islands. Some elements had to be retained in the region of the Magellan Straights to deter any temptation to intervene on the part of the Chilean Navy and in this respect and contrary to Argentine propaganda reports the two German-built 'Indómita' and four Israeli-built 'Dabur' class fast attack craft remained in this region throughout the conflict. The ancient cruiser *General Belgrano* and the destroyers *Bouchard* and *Piedrabuena* were also earmarked to provide a back-up to this force.

The Air Force deploy — as much against Chile as the Task Force

The major units of the Air Force were however redeployed southwards to points from which they could both provide tactical support to the garrison of the Falklands and still continue to provide a deterrent to any Chilean intervention.

The Argentine Air Force actually had considerably fewer combat aircraft available for service than were indicated by intelligence reports. There were only 11 Mirages instead of 16 as generally believed, 46 Skyhawks instead of 65 and 6 Canberras instead of 9. There were however 34 Neshers rather than the 26 with which usually reliable sources credited the Fuerza Aérea Argentina.

As well as the Pucarás of the III Air Brigade, four

Argentine cruiser *Belgrano*, before she was sunk by British nuclear submarine, *Conqueror*. She was due for retirement and conversion into a naval museum.

Above: American-built A4 Skyhawk in service with the Argentine Navy during the war. Below: British-built Canberra bomber of the Argentine Air Force.

of the nine Beech T-34C Turbo Mentor strike trainers of the Navy's 4th Attack Squadron were already in the Falklands together with five of the ten Macchi MB.339s of the 1st Attack Squadron. The Navy also had two Lockheed Neptune maritime reconnaissance aircraft in the 1st Reconnaissance Squadron at Comandante Espora naval air base which also housed the five Super Etendard fighter-bombers of the 2nd Naval Fighter-Attack Squadron, the 11 Skyhawks of the 3rd Fighter-Attack Squadron and the six Grumman Trackers of the 1st Naval Anti-Submarine Squadron. Elements of the Skyhawk and Tracker squadrons were normally deployed aboard the *Veinticinco De Mayo* although the Super Etendards could not yet operate from the carrier.

Exocet training begins

Commander Jorge Colombo's 2nd Naval Fighter-Attack Squadron had only come into existence five months earlier and its pilots had a mere 45 hours experience in flying the Super Etendard at the time of the invasion. Commander Colombo received orders to commence training with the AM.39 air-to-surface version of the Exocet missile on 31 March, the day before the first assault troops went ashore at Port Stanley. Despite the withdrawal of French assistance, the naval air arm technicians rigged-up a launching system within two weeks.

Although no Super Etendards or other first-line jets ever attempted a normal landing or take-off from the Falklands, a facsimile of the main runway at Stanley airport was marked out at Comandante Espora naval air base and exercises were carried out which indicated that a Super Etendard could take off from Stanley in both wet and dry conditions but that the Stanley runway, even after the improvements carried out by the Argentine Army engineers, was too short for a landing in the wet. As this represented the most usual condition which might be expected over the next three months, the project of operating naval fighter-bombers from Stanley was abandoned. Exercises in refuelling in flight from the two KC-130 tankers of the Argentine Air Force were also carried out and by mid April a simulated attack on enemy warships in Falkland waters had been successfully accomplished. In all 55 extra flying hours were

Above: Exaggerated claims and retouched photographs added fuel to the propaganda war.

The 5 French-built Super Etendards bought by Argentina just after delivery to 2 Naval Fighter Attack Sqdn.

Above: An Argentine Air Force 4th Air Brigade A4 Skyhawk, with a silhouette of a British warship and a date, 30th May, below the cockpit. No Task Force ships were sunk that day, though *Exeter* was attacked. Left: AM-39 Exocet missile attached to underwing of French Super Etendard. French technicians did not supply Argentine engineers after hostilities began.

clocked up by the pilots of the 2nd Naval Fighter-Attack Squadron during the first half of April and on 19 April the Squadron re-deployed to Rio Grande.

The air war begins

On 2 May an attempted air strike by two Super Etendards had been aborted after difficulties with in-flight refuelling and the following day, one of the naval Macchis based at Stanley was lost accidentally during bad weather and its pilot killed. The Argentine anti-aircraft gunners drew their first blood two days later, downing a Harrier over Goose Green.

A Neptune of the First Naval Reconnaissance Squadron located the main body of the British Task Force at about 100 miles south of Stanley, early on 4 May, continuing to shadow it throughout the morning. Two Super Etendards took off from Rio Grande at 9.45 am, rendezvousing with a KC-130 15 minutes later and continuing eastwards after refuelling. Maintaining radio silence and guided by situation reports from the Neptune, which surprisingly was not attacked by the Harriers, the two Super Etendards continued flying eastwards until the first radar contact revealed a target. Without waiting for a visual siting, both aircraft launched their Exocets and headed for home. The first Exocet hit the destroyer *Sheffield*, causing fatal damage, the second missile narrowly missing the frigate *Yarmouth* and crashing harmlessly into the sea. The two Argentine aircraft returned safely to base.

ASSESSING THE PUCARÁ

As the only recent military combat aircraft of Argentine design, the IA 58A Pucará was naturally of particular interest, not only to Britain alone but in providing a yardstick of third-world expertise in a challenging field. The Pucará (the name is that of stone cairns or forts built by early Indians) was designed by the Fábrica Militar de Aviones as a Co-In (counter-insurgent) aircraft to quell uprisings by groups within Argentina itself. Its qualities fitted it well for participation in the Falklands fighting.

Powered by two 988-horsepower Turboméca Astazou 14G turboprops imported from France, it has a modest performance, well below that of a World War 2 Spitfire. Of course, it is not intended for air combat but to apply firepower accurately on ground targets, and have the best possible chance of surviving small-arms fire. It packs quite a punch, with two 20mm cannon and four machine guns firing ahead and the ability to carry up to 3,307lb (1500kg) of external weapons including individual bombs of up to 2,205lb (1000kg). It will be recalled that masses of napalm were found by British troops being packaged into aircraft drop tanks ready for use by these aircraft.

All the Pucarás in the islands were lost, and two were brought undamaged to Britain. One, previously aircraft A-515 of the Fuerza Aerea Argentina, was taken on the strength of the Ministry of Defence (Procurement Executive) with serial number ZD485, and after thorough overhaul was subjected to a brief programme of handling and performance measurements at Boscombe Down, the MoD Aeroplane & Armament Experimental Establishment. This was the first time in almost 40 years that Boscome had been called upon to study a captured aircraft. (During the Falklands campaign the establishment had been required to carry out 110 separate test programmes in ten weeks, including clearance of many new weapon fits and addition of AAR probes to the Hercules and Nimrod, both of which suffered handling problems as a result.)

Lightly loaded, the Pucará was found to have a quite sprightly takeoff, getting airborne in about 900ft (274m). In the air handling was pleasant, control response excellent and all-round visibility exceptional, except where blocked by the projecting engines and propellers. The Astazou runs at constant speed, and power is varied by altering fuel flow and propeller pitch, response being rapid. No attempt was made at aerobatics, but rate of roll was

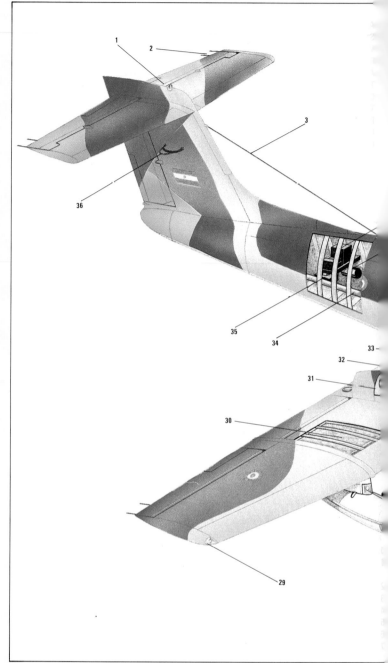

thought good for an aircraft of nearly 50ft (15m) span.

Thanks to the use of standard US Aero 7A-1 and 20A-1 stores pylons it was possible to load the aircraft up with various external loads. These made a considerable difference to takeoff run (it was soon found to be more than doubled) and all forms of performance and handling deteriorated. Weapon delivery was not attempted, but the French Matra optical sight is a well-known pattern and is adequate for its original purpose. The Pucará has no bad-weather capability, and in effect is basically World War 2 technology updated.

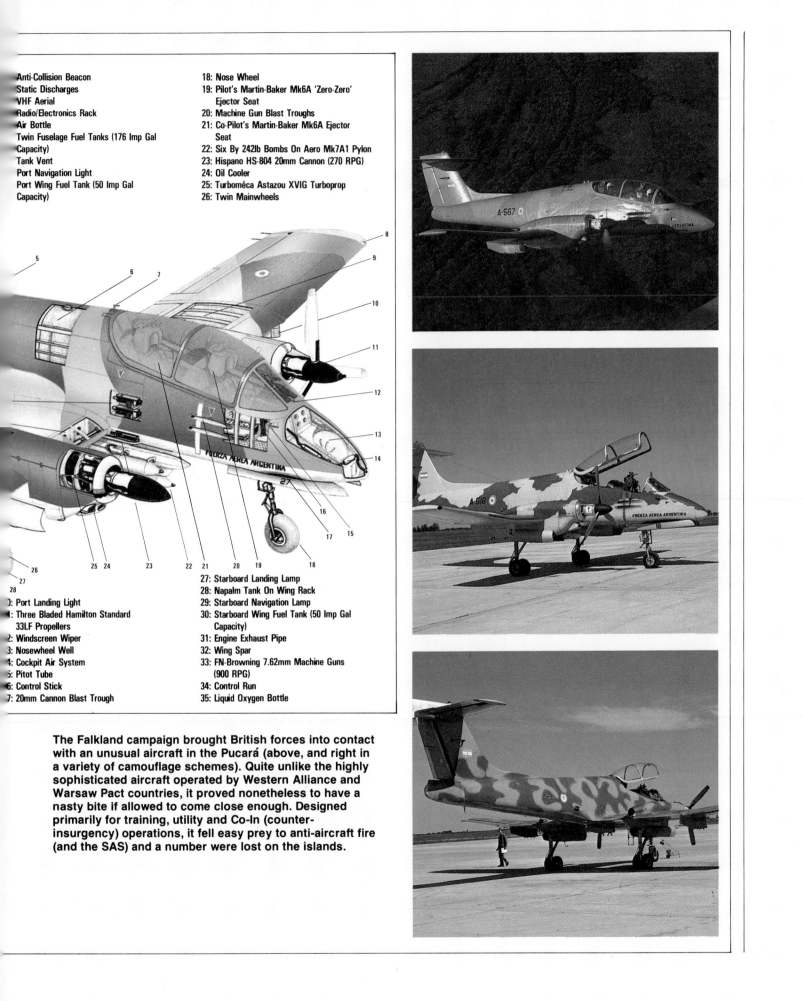

Anti-Collision Beacon
Static Discharges
VHF Aerial
Radio/Electronics Rack
Air Bottle
Twin Fuselage Fuel Tanks (176 Imp Gal
Capacity)
Tank Vent
Port Navigation Light
Port Wing Fuel Tank (50 Imp Gal
Capacity)

18: Nose Wheel
19: Pilot's Martin-Baker Mk6A 'Zero-Zero'
    Ejector Seat
20: Machine Gun Blast Troughs
21: Co-Pilot's Martin-Baker Mk6A Ejector
    Seat
22: Six By 242lb Bombs On Aero Mk7A1 Pylon
23: Hispano HS-804 20mm Cannon (270 RPG)
24: Oil Cooler
25: Turboméca Astazou XVIG Turboprop
26: Twin Mainwheels

27: Starboard Landing Lamp
28: Napalm Tank On Wing Rack
29: Starboard Navigation Lamp
30: Starboard Wing Fuel Tank (50 Imp Gal
    Capacity)
31: Engine Exhaust Pipe
32: Wing Spar
33: FN-Browning 7.62mm Machine Guns
    (900 RPG)
34: Control Run
35: Liquid Oxygen Bottle

0: Port Landing Light
1: Three Bladed Hamilton Standard
   33LF Propellers
2: Windscreen Wiper
3: Nosewheel Well
4: Cockpit Air System
5: Pitot Tube
6: Control Stick
7: 20mm Cannon Blast Trough

The Falkland campaign brought British forces into contact with an unusual aircraft in the Pucará (above, and right in a variety of camouflage schemes). Quite unlike the highly sophisticated aircraft operated by Western Alliance and Warsaw Pact countries, it proved nonetheless to have a nasty bite if allowed to come close enough. Designed primarily for training, utility and Co-In (counter-insurgency) operations, it fell easy prey to anti-aircraft fire (and the SAS) and a number were lost on the islands.

Naval activity after the Belgrano

The submarine *San Luís* was also in the vicinity of the *Sheffield* when the latter vessel was hit by the Exocet and fired one torpedo without effect at either HMS *Arrow* or *Yarmouth*, being prevented from firing further torpedoes by the presence of Sea King anti-submarine helicopters, one of which fired a Sting-Ray torpedo at the submarine, also without effect. The British Task Force now withdrew to beyond the range of mainland based aircraft, bad weather restricting further air strikes.

On 5 May a Tracker aircraft reported a possible submarine contact 180 miles east of Comodoro Rivadavia, where Task Group 79.1 was now located, a Sea King helicopter joining the hunt and dropping two torpedoes, apparently without effect. Shortly afterwards the carrier returned to Puerto Belgrano where her aircraft were disembarked, the eight Skyhawks, together with three spare aircraft from Comandante Espora naval air base, being redeployed to join the Super Etendards at Rio Grande.

Bad weather continued to hamper air activity although on 7 May the Argentine Air Force resumed transport flights between the mainland and Stanley which had been suspended following the air attacks of 1 May. Two days later the Argentine trawler *Narwal* was attacked by Harriers and Sea King helicopters 60 miles east of Stanley, one of her crew of 26 being killed and 14 wounded and the surviving members taken off by helicopter. An Army Puma helicopter was also shot down by a Sea Dart missile from *Coventry* and two Skyhawks of the IVth Air Brigade were lost on 9 May when they crashed in poor visibility on West Falkland whilst engaged in the only attempted Argentine air strike during this period.

Two days after that the transport *Isla De Los Estados*, laden with fuel and ammunition for the garrison of West Falkland, was surprised and sunk with all hands in Falkland Sound by the frigate *Alacrity*, the frigate evading a torpedo fired by the submarine *San Luís* at 1.30 am as she sailed back towards Stanley. The submarine then returned to base, its torpedoes being exhausted.

On the Falklands, the garrison in their waterlogged foxholes continued to endure regular naval bombardment, the field batteries emplaced in the vicinity of Stanley replying ineffectually. To relieve the ground forces of this constant harassment two flights, each of four Skyhawks of the Vth Air Brigade, took off from Rio Gallegos on 12 May to attack the British destroyer *Glasgow* and the frigate *Brilliant* which were then bombarding Stanley airfield. Two aircraft of the first wave, were shot down by Sea Wolf missiles, another also crashing as it took evasive action. Only one Skyhawk returned to base, suffering damage when it overran the runway on landing.

The second wave fared better, *Glasgow* being hit by a 1,000 pound bomb which whilst it failed to explode smashed through the hull causing sufficient damage to force her withdrawal to Ascension for repairs, another bomb bouncing harmlessly over *Brilliant*. Unfortunately, Lieutenant Gavazzi who had dropped the bomb which hit *Glasgow* fell a victim to his own anti-aircraft gunners as he flew over Goose Green on his way back to base. Although the mission resulted in the loss of 50% of the aircraft involved, together with their pilots, the damage to *Glasgow* and the narrow escape of *Brilliant* caused the British to suspend bombardment of Stanley airfield during the daylight hours.

Bad weather caused the suspension once more of combat air operations for the next three days and on the night of 14 May, Pebble Island, garrisoned by some naval aviation and Air Force personnel plus a company of the 3rd Marines suffered a raid by the SAS. The six Air Force Pucarás and the four naval T-34Cs stationed there were destroyed, together with a Skyvan of the Coast Guard, as were the two powerful radar stations located on the island.

On the night of 15 May, although combat flying remained restricted by weather conditions, an Air Force Hercules flew the first of three 155mm howitzers into Stanley. The following day the unarmed supply ship *Rio Carcaraña* was attacked by Harriers in Falkland Sound and so badly damaged that she had to be beached to avoid sinking. The armed transport *Bahía Buen Suceso*, at anchor in Fox Bay, drove off two air attacks with her anti-aircraft guns before finally suffering damage which caused her subsequent abandonment. A pair of Super Etendards mounted an abortive attack against the Task Force on 17 May, failing to make contact and returned intact to Rio Grande. There was little activity for the next few days although a fuel dump at Fox Bay was bombed by Harriers on 20 May.

The Argentine garrison in the islands prepares for the arrival of the Task Force

On the eve of the British re-invasion there were about 11,400 Argentine military personnel in the Falkland archipelago. At or in the vicinity of Stanley were the three infantry regiments (3rd, 6th and 7th) of the Xth Brigade; the 4th Infantry, many of whose members were already suffering the effects of their sudden transition from the sub-tropical climate of their normal station near the Brazilian frontier to the semi-Antarctic conditions of the Falklands in winter, and the 25th Infantry. There were also the 601st Commando Company, the 5th Marine Infantry Battalion, reinforced by a battery of six 105mm howitzers, a Marine Special Forces unit and elements of the 10th Armoured Cavalry Reconnaissance Squadron with 12 Panhard AML 245 H-90 armoured cars.

Argentine soldiers carry food supplies through Stanley: their colleagues in the hills were less fortunate.

Artillery support was provided by the 3rd Artillery Group, with eighteen 105mm howitzers and the similarly equipped 4th Airborne Artillery Group. There were also a battery of twin 35mm anti-aircraft guns from the 601st Anti-Aircraft Defence Group, a battery of single 30mm pieces and a Tigercat SAM battery, plus a Roland SAM unit from the Marine 1st Anti-Aircraft Regiment and an air defence battery of the Air Force with twin-mounted 20mm guns. The infantry also had British Blowpipe and Soviet SA-7 man-portable SAM launchers, the latter provided by Peru. Apart from logistic support and medical units, there was also the 10th Motorized Engineer Company and a company from the 601st Construction Engineer Battalion, together with a detachment from the 181st Military Police Intelligence Battalion. In addition to the 12 surviving Pucarás and the two examples apiece of the Chinook and Bell 212 helicopters of the Air Force and the 4 remaining naval Aermacchi 339s, based at Stanley airport, the Army had two Chinooks, two Pumas, three Agusta A-109 and nine Bell UH–1H and D helicopters in the vicinity of Stanley.

After Stanley, the main concentration of Argentine forces was at Goose Green where the 12th Infantry, together with half of a 105mm howitzer battery of the 4th Artillery Group plus a troop of 35mm A/A guns and a battery 20mm pieces manned by the Air Force, were deployed, together with about 200 Air Force personnel to operate the half dozen Pucarás based at the air strip. In overall command was an Air Force officer, Air Commodore Wilson Pedrozo, the more numerous army elements being under the command of Lieutenant-Colonel Halo Piaggi.

Other points on East Falkland were covered by small outposts, at not more than platoon strength, or by patrols. There were also still about 100 naval aviation and Air Force personnel and a company of the 3rd Marines on Pebble Island although the value of this installation had greatly diminished after the raid on 12 May.

West Falkland was garrisoned by the 5th Infantry at Port Howard and the 8th Infantry plus the 9th Combat Engineer Company at Fox Bay, the garrison being commanded by Brigadier General Parada with his HQ at Port Howard. As on East Falkland, no major troop concentrations occurred outside these two centres, the remainder of the Island being covered by desultory patrols. The only Argentine aircraft based on West Falkland were three army

Puma and one Agusta 109 helicopters, based at Port Howard.

Although the Argentine forces were well equipped, personal small arms tended to be badly maintained. Many of the FN FAL rifles which were the standard small arm of the Argentine infantry had been so neglected as to be almost useless. The Argentine PAM sub-machine gun, which was the standard light automatic, was also a mediocre weapon which came to be loathed and distrusted by the troops unfortunate enough to be equipped with it.

Those lucky enough to be billeted in Stanley itself or any of the lesser settlements enjoyed relatively comfortable living conditions. The less fortunate, who lived under canvas, suffered greatly from the cold, their uniforms rapidly proving inadequate for the Falkland climate in Winter whilst those actually manning the shallow field works, which were all that could be managed in terrain which was partly rock and partly bog, plumbed the depths of environmental misery. Sanitary arrangements tended to be primitive and haphazard, latrines being dug without regard to the location and most other ranks did not experience the luxury of a bath throughout the ten week long occupation. Inevitably sickness, particularly respiratory and rheumatic complaints attributable to the climate and intestinal ailments arising from defective hygiene, became widespread.

Although vast stocks of supplies had been built up during the first seven weeks of Argentine occupation, in practice, units located at any distance from the supply dumps often went hungry when rations failed to be distributed. Some of the conscripts begged food from the Kelpers, with varying results. The more enterprising shot and butchered sheep.

The Argentine Army had come under strong German influence from the turn of the century until after World War II and although US influence had begun to be felt from the late 1940s onwards, Prussian attitudes died hard. Officers, the NCOs, who formed the regular cadre and the twelve-month conscripts who provided the bulk of the manpower formed three separate, mutually exclusive and to a certain extent hostile groups. Officers tended to divorce themselves from their men and the day-to-day command functions normally discharged by junior officers in the British and United States Armies devolved upon NCOs. Discipline was brutal, punishments such as spread-eagling for long periods being frequently meted out for minor misdemeanours.

The relationships between officers and other ranks and morale and discipline in general were far superior in the Navy, which derived many of its traditions from British rather than German origins and in the Air Force and Marines which had come under strong United States influence. The best

Argentine land unit in the islands was undoubtedly Commander Carlos Robacio's 5th Marine Infantry Battalion. This was the Argentine Marine Corps's Antarctic warfare unit and although 80% of its personnel were conscripts, compared favourably with the British units with which it was soon to come into contact. Naval bombing was also disproportionately successful, the naval pilots (unlike the Air Force) having training in attacking shipping.

The British return, and the occupier's military prowess is put to the test

The British landings at San Carlos Bay went almost unopposed. Pre-war Argentine studies had dismissed San Carlos as a site for a landing and the settlement was garrisoned only by a reinforced platoon from the 12th Infantry Regiment which retreated in the face of the invaders, shooting down two Royal Marine Gazelle helicopters as they withdrew.

An SAS raid at Goose Green on the night of 20 May had largely occupied the attention of the defenders and the first real reaction to the landing at San Carlos came at 10am when a single Pucará flew a reconnaissance mission over the landing force, followed by a

Above: RFA logistic landing ship *Sir Galahad* under air attack in San Carlos Bay, the attacker a Mirage from VIth Air Brigade.

Above: An Argentine Mirage fighter-bomber climbs away to avoid anti-aircraft fire from a Rothsay class frigate, possibly *Plymouth*.

naval Macchi which carried out a bombing attack, causing some damage to the frigate *Argonaut*. Half an hour later an attack by six Neshers of the VIth Air Brigade resulted in damage to the destroyer *Antrim* and the frigate *Broadsword* for the loss of one aircraft. At noon an abortive attack by two Pucarás from Goose Green resulted in the loss of one aircraft although its pilot ejected safely and walked back to the airstrip.

The next Argentine air strike, by four Skyhawks of Vth Air Brigade, was dogged by ill-fortune, two aircraft having to turn back with fuel problems, a third wasting its bomb load on the wreck of the *Rio Carcaraña* in Falkland Sound and only the fourth succeeding in pressing home an attack on the frigate *Ardent*. A second wave of four Skyhawks from the IVth Air Brigade, were intercepted by Harriers over West Falkland, two being destroyed, one of the others making for home without completing its mission and the fourth releasing its bombs at *Ardent* without effect.

Ordeal for Ardent

The Neshers of VIth Air Brigade now returned to the attack, four aircraft being intercepted by Harriers short of their target and all being eventually shot down although not before causing further damage to *Ardent*. Meanwhile six Skyhawks of the Vth Air Brigade attacked *Argonaut* with relative impunity, also causing serious damage and again hitting *Ardent* before all withdrew safely. The Skyhawks of the 3rd Naval Fighter Attack Squadron now made their first appearance, three aircraft delivering the coup de grâce to the stricken *Ardent*. All three aircraft were destroyed, one as it attempted a forced landing at Stanley, although two of the three pilots ejected safely. Another flight of three naval Skyhawks attacked without effect at dusk and returned to base without suffering any damage or casualties.

At the bases on the mainland ground crews worked feverishly to repair damaged aircraft. Missile damage generally proved fatal. Aircraft which returned to base safely had usually suffered only

minor damage from gunfire and almost invariably were back in action the following day. Over the next few days Argentine pressure built up and fatal hits were scored on both *Coventry* and *Atlantic Conveyor*. *Sir Bedivere*, *Sir Galahad* and *Sir Launcelot* were also attacked in San Carlos Water.

From Goose Green to Stanley: the British breakout

The first major contact between the opposing ground forces came on the night of 27 May when patrols clashed north of Darwin. The Argentine patrols fell back upon Darwin where the bulk of their forces were entrenched in positions carefully but unimaginatively prepared in strict accordance with military text books. Although outnumbering their attackers, they had been already softened up by bombardment from HMS *Arrow*, later reinforced by air strikes. From first light their own Pucarás flew continuous ground attack missions against the advancing British, three falling victim to ground fire although two pilots ejected safely. The naval Macchis from Stanley also flew at least one ground support mission, one aircraft being shot down by a Blowpipe missile and its pilot killed.

On the ground the British paratroops advanced using the shock troop tactics perfected by the Germans in the latter stages of World War I. The imaginative but highly unorthodox use of anti-tank rockets and Milan missiles for trench-clearing caused terror amongst the defenders and in spite of an unsuccessful counterattack Darwin had surrendered by mid-morning. The advance had however slowed down by mid afternoon and ground almost to a halt with the approach of darkness. Argentine demoralization was fairly complete

however and before hostilities could resume the following day, Air Commodore Pedrozo, commanding the garrison, requested a parley and later in the morning approximately 900 Army and 200 Air Force troops surrendered. Argentine losses had been approximately 50 dead and not 250 as indicated by contemporary reports, plus 150 wounded.

Stanley began to come under heavy air attack from 30 May. Naval bombardment once more became a regular occurrence although a Harrier fell victim to small arms fire at noon on 30 May. At about the same time two Super Etendards, one of them carrying the sole remaining Exocet missile, the other to provide back-up radar cover, escorted by four Skyhawks of the IVth Brigade, attacked the outer screen of the British Task Force from the south-east, having re-fuelled twice during the extended flight from Rio Gallegos. As usual, the Super Etendards headed for home after launching their missile load which exploded before scoring a hit, two of the Skyhawks also falling victims to anti-aircraft missile fire before reaching the target area. The remaining two Skyhawks claimed hits on both the destroyer *Exeter* and the frigate *Avenger*.

Little activity occurred on 31 May but on the following day four Canberras made a bombing attack on Port San Carlos, returning to base safely. Deteriorating weather hindered aerial combat operations and prompted an increase in supply flights into Stanley and a Hercules which was foolhardy enough to attempt a reconnaissance sweep on its homeward flight was shot down by Harriers with the loss of its seven occupants. The anti-aircraft gunners at Stanley however extracted rapid revenge, shooting down a Harrier although its pilot ejected and was later rescued by a British helicopter.

The Argentine Air Force mounted its first major air strike for over a week on 8 June when six Neshers of the VIth Brigade and eight Skyhawks of the Vth took off to attack the landing force at Fitzroy. Five of the Skyhawks failed to refuel in flight and had to return to base as did a Nesher which developed an oil leak but the remainder pressed on. The five remaining Neshers encountered HMS *Plymouth* in Falkland Sound, expending their bomb load on the frigate which suffered considerable damage before turning for home at the approach of a flight of Harriers. The five remaining Skyhawks had meanwhile attacked the landing ships *Sir Galahad* and *Sir Tristram* at Fitzroy, causing fatal damage to the former and severely damaging the latter before heading back to base. At 5 pm four more Skyhawks of the IVth Brigade carried out another strike, this time being forced to withdraw with damage from smallarms fire. Just before dusk three Skyhawks of the Vth Brigade attacked and sank a landing craft in Choiseuil Sound but all fell victims to the avenging Harriers.

Above: Firefighting aboard *Sir Tristram* in Bluff Cove during an Argentine air attack on 8 June. Above, left: *Sir Galahad* ablaze at anchor off Fitzroy after Skyhawk attack on 31 May.

Below: *Plymouth* burning in the Falkland Sound after the 8 June air attack by VIth Air Brigade Neshers, the first major air attack for a week involving a force of fourteen aircraft. Alongside is *Avenger*.

The battle for Stanley and the final defeat

Although Stanley was now under almost continuous naval bombardment little contact had occurred between the opposing land forces since Goose Green. On 10 June a brisk fire-fight took place between a section of the 602nd Commando Company and British Marines at Top Malo House north-west of Stanley, the seven Argentine survivors only surrendering after their nine comrades had been killed and their ammunition exhausted. At about this time two Exocet launchers, dismounted from the damaged frigate *Guerrico*, were flown into Stanley and mounted on a trailer. On 12 June one of the two remaining airworthy naval Skyhawks bombed Darwin before withdrawing safely after the arrival of two Harriers and the battle for Stanley commenced in earnest.

General Menéndez had deployed the 4th Infantry on Two Sisters ridge, Mount Harriet and Mount Kent, to the west of Stanley. The 7th Infantry, reinforced by one of the Special Forces units, held Mount Longdon and Wireless Ridge, to the north, whilst the 5th Marines were responsible for the defence of Tumbledown, Mount William and Sapper Hill to the south. The 25th Infantry held Stanley airport and the beaches to the south-east, considered the most likely site for a British landing. A company of the 6th Infantry Regiment occupied the ridge between Two Sisters and Mount Longdon, another company, together with a company of the 1st Infantry completing the defensive line to the south-east and the 3rd Infantry was deployed to the south of Sapper Hill.

The bulk of the 4th Artillery Group was stationed to the west of Stanley, with one battery sharing Stanley racecourse with a battery of the 3rd Artillery, a battery of the latter unit being also based at Moody Brook barracks. The anti-aircraft units were deployed in the vicinity of Stanley itself and at the airport, the armoured vehicles and heavy artillery being held in reserve in the town. B Company of the 7th Infantry on Mount Longdon were quickly overrun, a counter-attack by C Company bogging down at 2 am. Meanwhile, B Company of the 4th Infantry was overrun on Mount Harriet. Throughout the day most of the remaining Argentine positions held, snipers from the 601st Commando Company proving particularly deadly to the British in the Sapper Hill sector. On Two Sisters C company of the 4th Infantry was however overrun, the bulk of the Regiment holding. However by sundown Goat Ridge and Mount Wall had also fallen. Whilst these engagements were in progress an Exocet was launched from the improvised trailer, causing serious damage to HMS *Glamorgan* which was bombarding Stanley.

The following day eight Skyhawks of the Vth Brigade set out from Rio Gallegos, one having to

return with engine trouble but the remaining seven carrying out an effective bombing attack on the British ground forces at Mount Kent, narrowly missing their brigade headquarters. That night the surviving Canberras also made a bombing attack on Mount Kent, losing one of their number to a missile from *Exeter* as they headed for home. The night of 13 June also saw the last Hercules flight in and out of Stanley. During the 37 days since the resumption of transport flights the C-130s of the Air Force had made 31 supply runs into Stanley and two parachute drops to other parts of the islands, carrying 400 tons of equipment and evacuating 264 wounded. During the same period, the Navy's Electras and Fellowships flew a similar number of sorties, carrying in 70 tons of equipment and 340 personnel as reinforcements. Throughout the entire campaign the Air Force made 420 transport flights between the mainland and Stanley and the Navy 59, an average of more than six flights a day.

The defensive line was now contracting and Wireless Ridge, held by the remnants of the 7th Infantry Regiment and a company of the 3rd Infantry, reinforced by the 10th Armoured Cavalry Reconnaissance Squadron, fighting as infantry, came under attack and despite a counter-attack had been forced to yield ground by dawn on 14 June. The 5th Marines, holding the slopes of Mount Tumbledown, were now surrounded on three sides, providing a most tenacious resistance although after an unsuccessful counterattack they were forced to withdraw to Sapper Hill. Most of the Argentine artillery was by now out of action, the British light guns having a 50% greater range than their Oto Melaras and being able to pick them off with impunity. The remnants of the Marines on Sapper Hill were virtually surrounded by 10 am and were forced to retreat.

With the British occupying all of the high ground around Stanley the inner defensive line now broke, demoralized troops leaving their positions and streaming into the town. Further resistance was hopeless and at 8.59 pm General Menéndez formally surrendered the surviving 10,254 Argentine troops in the islands. During the campaign the Argentines had suffered 1,241 killed and 1,046 wounded.

Summary

The performance of the Argentine Army, if undistinguished, was better than contemporary British accounts would indicate, bearing in mind that the troops which faced them — Guards, Ghurkas, SAS,

**Above, left: The final phase — Argentine prisoners taken by men of 2 Para after the battle for Mount Longdon.
Below, left: Under Royal Artillery supervision, Argentine troops discard their weapons and ammunition after the final surrender.**

Spoils of war: captured Argentine Air Force twin Oerlikon on display in England after the war.

Paratroops and Royal Marines — were the elite of one of the world's finest armies, with a history of almost continuous combat experience since the end of World War II.

Undoubtedly the considerable ferocity with which the campaign was pursued by the British also had an adverse effect on the morale of an opponent whose motivation was already faltering. The Ghurkas in particular excited an irrational terror in largely teenage conscripts who faced them and the shock troop tactics used by the British came as an unpleasant surprise to an enemy who had not fought a war against a foreign enemy for 112 years and who tended to fight strictly by the instruction manual.

Whilst low morale was undoubtedly a factor in the Argentine defeat, incompetent leadership was an even more potent one. The deployment of troops was unimaginative and units frequently operated with little co-ordination, once in position tending to sit and wait to be attacked rather than engage in a mobile defence.

The performance of the Navy was probably less undistinguished than would appear from contemporary British accounts. The withdrawal of the major Argentine surface units following the sinking of the *Belgrano* was prudent in the face of at least three British nuclear attack submarines and the maintenance of a 'fleet in being' when confronted by a greatly superior adversary has numerous historical precedents.

The performance of the Argentine Air Force and Naval Aviation and their suicidal bravery as they continued to attack in the face of crippling losses was impressive by any standards. Were it not for the high proportion of bombs which failed to explode, the losses of ships from air attack alone could well have forced the Task Force to withdraw. As it was, many of the British ships were hit by bombs or missiles, 4 major surface warships, 2 landing ships and a large container ship being sunk and at least 4 other destroyers and frigates, a third landing ship, and three supply ships seriously damaged.

The successes of the Argentine air forces were, however, achieved at enormous cost. 13 Mirage/Neshers were destroyed of 45 available at the beginning of hostilities; 22 Skyhawks of 57 of this type in the Air Force and Navy; 2 of the 6 remaining Canberras; 14 of the 75 available Pucarás; 2 of the Navy's 10 Aermacchi MB.339s shot down and 19 helicopters destroyed, in addition to a C-130 transport and 2 Skyvans of the Coast Guard.

Prospects

By mid 1984 the Argentine Armed Forces had more than made good their losses of equipment in the Falklands War.

The Aviation Command of the Argentine Army announced, during the second part of 1983, that it was to form a Mobile Assault Brigade, the major airlift capacity of which was to be provided by 24 Super Puma helicopters.

Three of the new Meko Type 360 destroyers had already entered service with the Navy and another was delivered later in 1984. The first of the six projected MEKO 140 light frigates was also in service and a second was due for launching during the first half of 1984 although two sister ships were still in an early stage of construction and work had not even commenced on two more projected vessels. One of the six projected Type TR 1700 submarines was delivered towards the end of 1983 and the second was due for delivery in 1984. In May 1984 Argentina was also reputedly negotiating the purchase of French nuclear power plants for at least two of the four additional projected submarines and for the transfer of an existing French nuclear-powered submarine.

The last four of the 14 Super Etendards on order were shipped from France in December 1983 and the Aviación Naval acquired 24 second-hand Skyhawks from Israel which more than compensated for the combat attrition during the Falklands War. Ten additional MB.339 and 12 Embraer Xavante light strike aircraft were also received during 1983. The Navy was also converting its three Lockheed Electra transports into long-range maritime reconnaissance aircraft and had acquired three more examples from commercial sources.

The combat strength of the Air Force during the first half of 1984 included 129 Mirage and Nesher fighter-bombers, 34 Skyhawks and 56 Pucarás.

The Argentine Navy and Air Force are already immensely more powerful than they were in 1982 and all three of the armed forces must have learned many valuable lessons during the Anglo-Argentine War. Although the Alfonsín Government announced its intention of pursuing the Falklands dispute by diplomatic means after it replaced the military Junta in December 1983, failing a diplomatic solution of the Falklands problem, eventually there will almost certainly be another Anglo-Argentine military confrontation. It may have a different outcome, if the lessons aren't applied.

Top: Repatriated Argentine prisoners return home after their Government finally allowed the Royal Navy to land them. Right: New Argentine Navy MEKO warship, *Almirante Brown*, on sea trials in the North Sea.

Chapter 6

BRITISH FORCES ABROAD: A GLOBAL ROLE

Despite the ever-shortening horizons of Empire, Britain's military presence still plays an important part in world peace-keeping. Guarding NATO's flanks, jungle-training in the tropics, mountaineering in the arctic circle or quelling distant rebellions — British servicemen can still expect to see overseas postings, and sometimes active service.

Jungle patrol in Belize report back to base by radio.

The Falklands conflict proved one thing probably above all others — that the British forces must be among the most adaptable and professional in the world. It was no small feat to be able to bring together three wings of the British forces, 8,000 miles from home in hostile weather conditions and to effectively sort out the enormous problems of logistics and supply into the bargain. Nevertheless, it happened and it happened in such a way as to give the British forces its biggest morale boost in the eyes of the world since the end of the Second World War. Less well known is the fact that British Forces have been sent overseas on *fighting* operations more than 90 times since 1945.

To many soldiers, sailors and airmen involved in Operation Corporate, the passage to the South Atlantic represented their first operation abroad of any magnitude. And it is this factor that is perhaps the most remarkable and reveals how changed the modern British serviceman has become.

There was a time, not long ago — perhaps 25 years — when it could still be said that the sun never set on the British Empire. The British had commitments all round the world and the Army in particular manned garrisons from Indonesia to the Caribbean. But these horizons have markedly diminished in the last quarter century and rapidly in the last 15 years with successive British governments showing an eagerness to withdraw all forms of British presence. Tight defence budgets and an increasingly important role in the western alliance in Europe has made such garrisons both expensive and politically embarrassing.

Ask any soldier nearing the end of a full career engagement about the number of postings abroad now available to his contemporaries as compared with the time he joined up. The answer will be the same in every case: there are now only five or six postings and the average short career soldier is unlikely to see more than the obvious one in Germany; there used to be more like 20 postings overseas. A soldier joining the Army on a six-year engagement is almost certainly going to serve in Germany, as is an airman joining the RAF, and a rating joining the Royal Navy will doubtless see Gibraltar at least once and probably stop in at some of the Mediterranean ports of call. Any more than this is increasingly uncertain. The British fighting forces' character and tradition is, in fact, established in overseas campaigns but the opportunities to reinforce this character have rapidly diminished. In some ways the Falklands experience was a recall to a former style of British military campaign but one relying heavily on a thoroughly professional force bringing new weapons and equipment to bear, often for the first time in operational use.

But despite the diminishing role of Britain's forces overseas, there are still very strong ties with 37

A patrol emerges from thick jungle in Belize, armed with US made M16 rifles and one General Purpose Machine Gun (GPMG), standard British issue.

widely dispersed Commonwealth Countries and 11 British Dependencies including the Falkland Islands — any one of which may call upon the British for assistance. And it is still possible although it cannot be guaranteed that a British soldier will spend time in khaki on a jungle patrol using much the same equipment and tactical deployment as his forbears of the Kipling era of Empire; or he may be training in arctic conditions in temperatures that can plummet into the minus 40s, or even be deployed in the mountainous terrains and deserts of Southeast Asia or the African continent. And it is possibly this degree of readiness and versatility for service anywhere in the world — the Royal Artillery's motto 'Ubique' meaning everywhere wasn't coined for any indulgent reason — that brought the Falkland's campaign to such a successful conclusion.

NATO comes first

Britain's defence commitment to the North Atlantic Treaty Organization is uppermost in defence planning and manpower organisation but, as outlined

in the Defence White Paper in June 1984, Britain's defence effort beyond the NATO area still operates on three levels:
'. . . the provision of military assistance and training to countries of importance to Western interest, which request our help; periodic deployment of British forces, including the deployment of naval task groups and exercises; and maintenance of a capability to intervene either to protect our national interest or, with allies and in response to a request for help, to protect those of the West as a whole. In addition we make an important contribution to international peace-keeping operations.'

Sometimes the operations have involved only a small troop of joint service personnel specially selected to support a Commonwealth ally. Sometimes this has involved a crackforce such as the Special Air Service or Special Boat Squadron deployed on counter-insurgency operations against guerrillas threatening countries whose stability is vital to British interests. But each one of these overseas operations has represented the furtherance of the British military experience overseas — an experience that is still nurtured in the few military outposts and garrisons left. These outposts, namely Gibraltar and Cyprus within the NATO

Mediterranean command, Hong Kong and Brunei in the Far East, and Belize in Central America, all have a questionable future in terms of a continued British presence. In the light of Britain's NATO commitment in western Europe, particularly in Germany, these outposts of empire have been streamlined to a bare minimum of resource in terms of manpower and equipment. As economic priorities are shuffled and re-evaluated these garrisons often suffer budget cuts and further paring; even a small garrison such as Belize operates at an enormous cost to the tax-payer.

Alongside the shrinking horizon of British military enterprise overseas, the Services themselves have changed rapidly in the last 25 years. The Army is now only a third of the size it was in the '50s. What was then a largely conscript force of men doing two years National Service, is now a totally professional regular Army with most members learning a trade that equips him for civilian employment once his engagement is up. The Navy has more than a hundred different trade employments and with increasingly sophisticated technology involved in military tasks, the character of the British serviceman from the lowest ranks upwards is changing from the once easily defined private soldier whose life usually comprised a tedious round of drill, parade and battle-fitness training, to a highly educated and specialist-trained individual coming from a wider cross-section of society than ever before. The increasingly technical nature of the Army alone accounts for the enormous expansion of numbers in the Royal Mechanical and Electrical Engineers, representing nearly ten in every 100 soldiers in the modern British Army in a Corps that was born in the last war to cope with the problems attendant on mechanized warfare. And with the Royal Artillery using such equipment as the Position and Azimuth Determining computer, laser range-finding equipment (also employed in the tanks of the Royal Armoured Corps), radar instrumentation for surface-to-air Rapier missiles, Royal Marines using Milan anti-tank guided missiles, and with a largely mechanized infantry travelling in heavily protected armoured personnel carriers, it is hardly surprising that the character, lifestyle and horizons of the Army have changed.

Recruitment has changed too. With the large number of unemployed at a time when British forces are enjoying renewed prestige — both as a result of the Falklands conflict and because of the heavily promoted professional image of the modern serviceman — there is a large number of high calibre candidates for each place. Instead of offering the once-applicable carrot of overseas travel and adventure, the recent recruitment literature has been able to report the exact nature of the jobs, outlining career advantages and even spelling out the occasional tedious routines of the work.

The NATO frontline

As mentioned above, today's soldier and airman will almost certainly spend some of his service career in Germany which is the frontline of British defences and headquarters of 1st British Corps in the British Army of the Rhine as well as four major RAF airfields. It is reckoned that many soldiers will in fact spend as much as two thirds of a short term engagement of six years in Germany where the 55,000 strong British force is a vital part of NATO's Northern Army Group. This covers the northeastern sector of the Warsaw Pact's western border. BAOR was initially a force gathered from the British forces occupying Germany after the war in 1946. It was then only two divisions strong and the manpower there has fluctuated according to the political temperature of East–West relations since then. In the late fifties, during the time of the Cold War, the 1st British Corps was formed and there were about 77,000 men. Since then the number has been kept to the minimum required by the various protocols of the Revised Brussels Treaty of 1954 — ie 55,000.

A separate Field Force with about 3,000 British troops is kept in Berlin and is not part of BAOR. In addition to the BAOR contingent — three armoured divisions and one artillery division — there is a newly formed rearguard force, the 5th Field Force with about 4,000 infantrymen. Altogether, with further troops and army personnel scattered in various NATO headquarters and at Emblem — a small village near Antwerp which is designated the main port of entry for British reinforcements in wartime — there are about 60,000 troops in Germany. This would more than double to about 150,000 with regular and reserve reinforcements during war.

BAOR is split into two main parts. The first is in Bielefeld with about 9,000 troops commanded by a lieutenant general and this is the Army's biggest operational command at present. Amongst other Corps housed there, the Royal Army Ordinance Corps operates a huge supply depot which provides vital back up supplies. The RAOC bakery, for example, can make up to 17,000 loaves in one full shift, and it operates round the clock supplying the various forces when they are on exercise. As a follow up to the last major allied exercise in Europe, Crusader in 1981, Operation Lionheart, in autumn 1984, involved the largest mass invasion of allied forces in Europe since 1945. Understandably the RAOC had a priority role in this. Part of its daily Bielefeld quota of provision is to feed 10,000 troops, this went up to nearer 25,000. The RAOC also holds war reserves and stocks and supplies petrol and rations to all the Rhine Army units and BFES schools in Germany as well as to the UK-based units

Where the forces are: a map showing the variety of countries playing host to the British military.

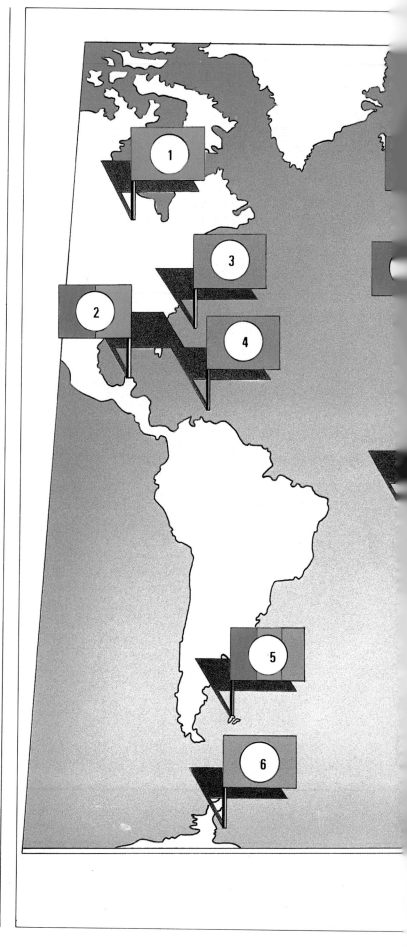

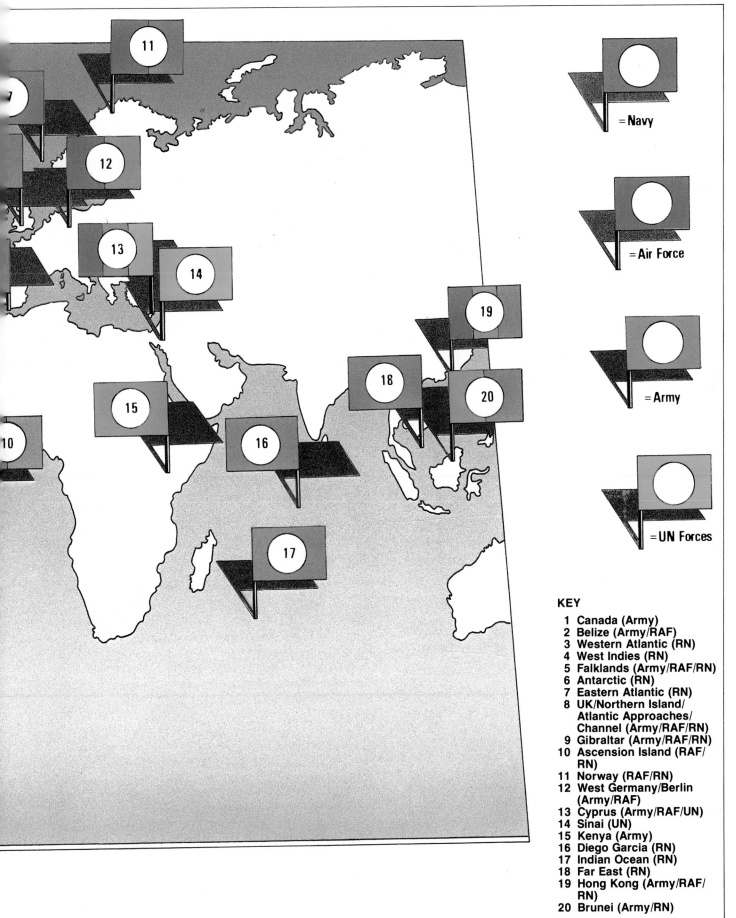

= Navy

= Air Force

= Army

= UN Forces

KEY

1 Canada (Army)
2 Belize (Army/RAF)
3 Western Atlantic (RN)
4 West Indies (RN)
5 Falklands (Army/RAF/RN)
6 Antarctic (RN)
7 Eastern Atlantic (RN)
8 UK/Northern Island/
   Atlantic Approaches/
   Channel (Army/RAF/RN)
9 Gibraltar (Army/RAF/RN)
10 Ascension Island (RAF/
   RN)
11 Norway (RAF/RN)
12 West Germany/Berlin
   (Army/RAF)
13 Cyprus (Army/RAF/UN)
14 Sinai (UN)
15 Kenya (Army)
16 Diego Garcia (RN)
17 Indian Ocean (RN)
18 Far East (RN)
19 Hong Kong (Army/RAF/
   RN)
20 Brunei (Army/RN)

operating in Germany. Other RAOC units hold and maintain stocks of the main (A and B) vehicles, towed guns and equipment, some of which are kept in protective envelope storage to shore them against the quite harsh German winters without the necessity of using buildings. In Gutesloh, another RAOC company holds motor and technical spares and a limited range of general stores.

Perhaps the RAOC's most unusual role is providing field shower units each of which can provide facilities for 120 men each hour to wash on exercise. The ROAC are in fact one of the Army's most essential back-up units, fundamental to the Army's defensive potential in time of war, a fact more than ever proved in the Falklands when supply was at once essential and almost impossible.

Each of the main divisions making up 1st British Corps has two armoured regiments with Chieftain tanks, one armoured reconnaissance regiment; three mechanized infantry battalions with armoured personnel carriers; a close-support artillery regiment with Abbot 105mm self-propelled guns, a battery of Swingfire anti-tank guns (to be replaced with multi launch rocket systems); one medium range general support artillery regiment with two batteries of M-109 155mm self-propelled guns and a battery of M-110 203mm howitzers — which can fire nuclear as well as conventional shells — and a battery of Blowpipe anti-aircraft missiles; one Army Air Corps regiment with 24 helicopters, half of which are Lynx helicopters armed with American Tow anti-tank missiles; and a REME regiment. These three

WHERE ARE THEY NOW?
Lt David Stewart, MC, Royal Marines

By the time he left university in 1980 David Stewart had already been in the Royal Marines for three years, and at 25 years of age he is now a confirmed 'lifer'. He originally joined in order to fly, but is now officially too old to learn, having decided instead to try for Signals Officer in 1985, a post which could give him more opportunities to go to different places and take part in a greater variety of operations. As soon as he returned from Falklands leave to Arbroath, where he was a member of X Company, Lt Stewart found himself scheduled to go to Northern Ireland.

"I was given a month to get my blokes together — 18 men — for a thing called Operation Interknit. It's basically for stopping smuggling operations on Carlingford Loch, smuggling operations and terrorists. It's near to Warren Point, where the Paras got done — in fact that was aimed at Operation Interknit. We patrolled both the Loch and the land. We checked all the ships as they came in, operating with one or two rigid raiding craft. Every ship that comes in has to slow down. We leap on the back and have a look inside. That goes on all the time. I was there until March of '83, with the same team of 18 marines. It was a four month tour, and we had to do a month's training beforehand, which included search courses. We had to do the normal pre-Northern Ireland training, and we did some raiding training with the ships. The search course was the main thing, the searching of vessels, and also of cars. It's mainly a deterrent, and to find something you've got to get a bit lucky. Nothing happened particularly interesting.

There's plenty of ordinary smuggling. They're very good at it. Poteen, and all sorts of other stuff. Poteen is excellent! If you get a good haul you drink it yourself. Anyone who's been to Northern Ireland will know what poteen is."

After his four month tour in Northern Ireland Lt Stewart returned to 45 Commando and worked as a training officer from March until October. His job was to co-ordinate much of the unit training, and involved booking the mountain areas in Scotland for the coming Christmas mountain training period, as well as preparing for the January Norway exercise. As a lifer he has his career prospects firmly in view. Age limits govern many possibilities in the services. 24 was the upper age limit for flying training, and promotion from captain to major in the Marines depends on completing the PQS 2, Professional Qualification Studies, which have to be carried out between the ages of 27 and 32. Beyond that age you stay a captain. Although David Stewart is still a lieutenant, he left Arbroath in October 1983 for the Royal Naval College at Dartmouth, to follow the Professional Studies Course, a voluntary course which gives a grounding in such things as strategic studies, international affairs, and weapons technology. The course is purely academic, and is not in itself a qualification, though it is useful to career officers with future staff examinations in their sights. In December 1983 Lt Stewart left Dartmouth for a new job, as a troop commander at Royal Marines Lympstone in Devon.

Training recruits in Lympstone
Lympstone is where aspiring Marine recruits succeed or fail in their quest for the coveted green beret. There are 40 men in a troop at Lympstone, and David Stewart and his NCOs stay with the same recruits from the day they come through the gates. "It's a 30 week training. That's the longest any

divisions have about 8,500 men in each, which would almost double to 14,000 in event of war. They would be deployed to fight in what is known as the Forward Combat Zone with the artillery division deployed where needed and the 5th Field Force operating behind the divisions to protect the flank and rear.

Once battle takes place — given, say, the example of a huge Russian invasion in this sector, it would be the work of the allied battle groups within these divisions to impede and break up the Russian advance — which in any event would comprise significantly more troops than any the allies could muster at any one point. In fact, the natural defence point in this part of Germany is the Rhine itself but the Germans have always been anxious to engage in confrontation further to the east which makes the

British and allies job that much harder. The various battle groups are structured so as to be as flexible in response to an invasion as possible, and each battle group contains smaller flexible units — the combat teams — comprising an assortment of the teeth arms.

For its part the RAF Strike Command is also based in Germany and is essential for a hard-line frontal attack on any invading Russian convoy. The RAF has greatly benefited from an extensive re-equipment programme in recent years, most noticeably with the introduction of the German/Italian/British Tornado aircraft. This extremely sophisticated fighter is already in service in Germany and there will be 385 in service by the end of the 1980s, making up half of the frontline of fighters. RAF fighter planes, including the Phantoms,

troops do anywhere. We get the raw recruit, the guy with the long hair. It takes us 30 weeks to get them into shape. They have to be up at 6 o'clock every morning. The first two weeks is the 'induction phase' during which they are not permitted to drop out, in case they are just feeling homesick or something. That has been preceded by a three day 'potential recruits course', which is a weeding out operation. Before we had it about 50% used to fail the full course, as we had no way of assessing them. There are two of these courses each week, each one needing a colour sergeant, a sergeant, and six corporals, plus the PT staff, all working full time on the new recruits. After the induction phase they are in the IMF — Initial Military Fitness, which is a course of Swedish PT. I think we're the only people who use Swedish PT now. It's gone out of fashion, but it's very good. It builds the person up into the sort of fitness that we need. They may be able to run further or faster before we get them, but afterwards they'll be able to do the things we want them to do, such as climb ropes and do assault courses with full kit on, in the times that are required for commando courses. It's very disciplined gymnastic work, very strict. When they pass out one of the things they have to do is to climb a thirty foot rope with full kit on. That's about 45lbs, plus a nine-pound rifle. In one period they may have to do that three or four times. You can't do that by brute strength. It has to be by climbing technique. They're not allowed to do it their own way. They have to do it the way we teach them. It's the only way to get to the top."

The IMF lasts for 10 weeks. Apart from the PT they are also going for free runs, swimming at the beach, and doing weapons training. They play games with names like 'murder ball'. David Stewart obviously relishes this aspect of training.

"There's one particularly interesting game where they go for a mud run. The stretch of water down

here reveals a marvellous expanse of black sludgey mud when the tide goes out. They love it. Well, we tell them they love it anyway. You're sinking down to just above your knees, and you're playing rugby in it. It's pretty soul destroying, but great fun. It takes days and days to get the sand out of your kit."

Along with the play comes the real work. Apart from fitness training is weapons training, with the SLR, the self loading rifle also used by the Paras, and the General Purpose Machine Gun (GPMG). The Light Machine Gun (LMG) used in Norway is taught separately. At around week 26 or 27 they begin the 4 week Commando course unique to the regiment. It goes in phases. There is the Defence Phase, and there is a Counter Revolutionary Operations Phase, also unique to the Marines. There is also a Patrolling Phase. "They're continuing to increase their fitness all the way through. Never a day passes without some form of PT. It gets bloody tough. They'll get up in the morning and be able to think about nothing except BFT — battle fitness training. The IMF is hard but enjoyable. But the BFT, on the bottom field where the assault course is, is bloody hard work."

Lt Stewart and his NCOs do the final tests along with their trainees, including the nine mile speed march in ninety minutes in full kit, and a final thirty mile march in seven hours. In a massive final exercise the recruits are out in bivouacs for nine days, advancing from Poole to Plymouth, with helicopter attacks and ambushes en route.

Lt Stewart will be training Marine recruits until December 1984 before going on to new things. When asked how long he is in for he is reluctant to compute a figure, because he simply cannot imagine leaving the regiment.

"I'm 25 years old now. I envisage being in the Marines until they don't want me or I don't want them." You get the impression that that will be a great many years in the future.

British army armoured vehicles during a NATO exercise in West Germany. The bulk of British forces are committed to the defence of Europe against Warsaw Pact aggression.

Jaguars, and Lightnings, boast precision guided and very sophisticated communications and weapons technology coupled with high-speed mobility. The new laser-guided bombs enable the aircraft to bring pin-point accuracy and lethality on strategic targets. But the key characteristic of the RAF's contribution is its flexibility and its ability to switch from a conventional to a nuclear role if necessary. At present RAF and allied air forces intend to match the Russians numerical air superiority with the high quality of the aircraft and pilots in these forces. Fighter planes can be ready to go to war within a very short time of the first indications of Warsaw pact intentions which makes them a viable deterrent in all events.

On the ground the RAF Regiments protect the military airfields with Rapier and Bloodhound surface-to-air missiles.

So much for theory. In fact, the Army is continually beset with problems of overstretching its resources, with problems of maintaining an enormous amount of machinery and equipment which requires very specialist training, with the problems of too much hardware and too few men to operate, and then there's the logistics and transport operation of getting nearly 77,000 dependent women and children away from the battle zone while about the same number are being flown in. RAF resources would be stretched to breaking point.

On a day-to-day operational basis the BAOR and RAF servicemen have to contend with problems of boredom and often lack of really effective employment because there is heavy restriction placed on the times when the British Army is allowed to exercise; there are also petrol restrictions applied to each vehicle with the tanks and guns having quotas of what's known as tracked mileage of as little as 300 miles a year. There are only fifteen weeks a year allocated for field exercise training which has to be shared between the various divisions of BAOR. As the commander of 1st British Corps has said "It is rather like trying to maintain the zeal and morale of men who are going to win Saturday's match, whilst hoping that the match is never played."

Germany is in fact a peculiar extension of Britain with troops and their wives staying within the confines of the extremely well appointed British bases and not mixing much with the local German communities. It is still in fact only a small percentage of soldiers and airmen who bother to learn the native tongue in a country in which they may spend a number of years.

Hong Kong — thirteen years to go

Best known for its bustling commercial empire, cheap electrical goods and made-to-measure suits, Hong Kong was leased to the British in 1898 and there are now only 13 years before that lease is up. The Chinese show no signs of unhappiness at the prospect of restoring this extraordinarily profitable capitalist centre to their own dominions. And when the bell finally tolls there will doubtless be a demand on their part that all signs of a British military presence leaves as well.

In fact the British forces in Hong Kong have already been pared to the bone in recent years. Under the 1975 Defence Costs Agreements Britain withdrew one infantry battalion, an artillery regiment and an armoured reconnaissance battalion, making up the rest into one brigade — or Field Force — where there had formerly been two. With this reduction in size the likelihood of a posting to Hong Kong is rapidly diminishing, especially for those servicemen of short engagements. And along with the Army, the RAF and Navy contingents were also reduced.

At the beginning of 1984 the total forces included Royal Navy patrol craft and a Royal Marines rigid raider squadron; one RAF squadron of eight Wessex helicopters and one Army Air Corps Squadron; four Gurkha Infantry Battalions and one Gurkha

Royal Marine rigid raiding craft alongside a junk off the coast of Hong Kong. Despite these efforts, huge numbers of illegal immigrants find their way into the country.

Engineer regiment; and one UK Infantry Battalion. The three Services divide and share the military task with the Gurkhas taking the greatest proportion of the workload.

There are now a little over 7,500 soldiers in Hong Kong which alone counts for over 90 per cent of the British presence, and 5,500 of this number are Gurkhas housed in their main recruit-training headquarters in Sek Kong in the sprawling New Territories area of the Chinese mainland. It is this area that demands the most of the British forces in Hong Kong and until recently has been an area of intermittent tension between Britain and the People's Republic.

Making the British Army's force seem even more apologetic the UK Infantry Battalion is stationed discretely on the southern side of Hong Kong Island some half hour's drive from the capital. Built originally to ward off pirates it is not the favourite or most comfortable of overseas postings in terms of accommodation.

Also included in the overall military presence is a force of about 1,000 locally recruited Chinese who never move away from the colony. There is, finally, a

A Royal Marine questioning a Hong Kong junk owner with the aid of an interpreter during a routine search for illegal immigrants or contraband.

body of men called the Royal Hong Kong Regiment which is run along the lines of a Territorial Army force with the volunteers trained and organised by regular British senior NCOs and officers who fill the key posts.

The British forces have several rôles in Hong Kong, the least convincing of which is to deter the colony from being overrun by the Chinese People's Liberation Army looking to take back what they consider to be British-occupied China before the lease expires. Apart from the fact that there would be very little that such a small British force could do about such an action, it is very unlikely. The Chinese are merely biding their time and behaving strictly within the bounds of the agreement.

The most important British role is working as a back-up to the police, a proportion of which are British-recruited. In 1967 Hong Kong suffered terrible riots as a result of an overspill of the Cultural Revolution and subsequently troops and police have maintained a 12-hour alert with all the trappings of Northern Ireland's anti-riot equipment at their disposal, including CS gas, water cannons, and Saracen armoured personnel carriers.

Until quite recently most troops stationed in Hong Kong were involved in a lot of community relations work. They ran youth camps, built roads and even fetched and carried water during one of the droughts — one of the vicissitudes of an otherwise quite pleasant climate providing you can put up with very humid heat. These activities have been cut in the main part because of the expense of man-time with reduced forces . . . British forces tend to keep their own company and that of the 6,000 wives and children who join the married men on this posting.

Probably the most exciting and demanding role in Hong Kong is looking out for illegal immigrants. One battalion at a time guards the 21-mile border dividing the New Territories from the Chinese mainland and each battalion on duty does a four to six week stint in field operation conditions.

The border is a slightly improvised affair denoted in some places by sentries on patrol, at others by a wire fence. At another point in the eastern sector it runs straight down the middle of the main street of a town called Sha Tau Kok. Tension is often caused when a soldier finds himself in Chinese territory. On one occasion a Gurkha soldier crossed the street to a stall to buy himself some underpants and was quickly surrounded by Chinese militia troops who kept him prisoner for several hours before official channels of communication secured his release.

Normally the duty battalion sets up its headquarters in Fan Ling police station which is one of several Hong Kong Pol-Mil headquarters — the centres of joint military and police activities which have uniquely evolved in the colony. The border itself is divided into Central, East and West sections with the battalion spread along each section.

The illegal immigrants are a now famous problem in Hong Kong and there is not a British patrol that doesn't turn up a few uninvited characters. The immigration problem reached a peak in 1979 when there were as many as 1,000 a day coming across — and these were just the ones that were caught and fed back across the border to the Chinese who hold them in low regard but never harm them. The Hong Kong government are well aware of the service put in by British servicemen in capturing the immigrants because this uninvited population largely consist of misfits in China who become misfits in Hong Kong. A large proportion of criminal activity, petty thieving and violence is the result of immigrant populations who cannot find work in the colony. With a population of five million in the size of less than an English county, this is hardly surprising.

Most of the immigrants come through in the eastern sector — particularly where the town of Sha Tau Kok makes a breakthrough easy. Many get through to the shores of the New Territories and endeavour to swim to the main island. These are often spotted by the patrolling helicopters who radio

Jungle warfare training in Brunei and Belize underlines the ability — and intention — to deploy British forces outside the NATO North European theatre if necessary.

an alert to the Royal Marines Rigid Raiders or the Royal Navy Patrol Craft in the vicinity. The rigid raiders, now adapted to service in all parts of the world, can intercept the swimmers very quickly being able to travel at up to 30 knots and turn on a sixpence at high speed. British servicemen find the sight of the often impoverished, wet and hungry Chinese immigrants a pitiful one as a large number are rounded up into the Pol-Mil headquarters after each patrol. But they prefer the business of returning these immigrants to their inscrutable and reserved compatriots at the border than any shooting war that used to be the case in this area. And to the Army Air Corps and RAF helicopter squadrons, the operational patrols are far more interesting than routine ferrying and air-taxiing work.

Probably as a result of British efficiency at capturing the immigrants and the fact that the British lease has now not long to go, relations with the Chinese have been slowly and steadily improving. Both sides watch the other's daily routines and behaviour across the thin divide, taking note of military activity and training practice — an odd area where east and west suffer a reserved

exchange both biding their time until 1997.

For most British servicemen — and their wives — Hong Kong is reckoned to be a good posting. Within the reasonably comfortable service married quarters they live well but cannot, whatever rank, enjoy the high life of the colony as do compatriot business executives and bankers. You need an enormous salary to live well in Hong Kong. And the Local Overseas Allowances do not count for that much.

The Army, Navy and RAF now share an enormous custom-built joint service headquarters at HMS Tartar, probably the first and last built of its kind with the possible exception of any prospective joint service building in the Falklands Garrison. In matters of inter-service protocol there is a certain polite regard, especially in the Officer's Mess where the customs observed on successive dinner nights are alternatively Army and Navy. But life goes on, duties are performed, patrols made, and British military rule holds sway — but with a wary eye on the future.

Snakes and 'Guats' in Belize

Whilst Hong Kong is the last outpost of Empire to speak of, Belize is the last real jungle where British forces deploy in an operational role. But it is not the kind of posting sought after by any soldier in the know. Just south of Mexico on the Atlantic side of

British forces across the globe: Scorpion (front) and Scimitar (behind) armoured reconnaissance vehicles in Belize on hard ground. For footsoldiers on soft ground, an oil pipeline makes a suitable bridge for a British Army patrol (below). Above: Logistic landing ship unloads stores off the British sovereign base in Cyprus.

Central America, Belize offers the British soldiers patrolling the border arbitrarily dividing this country from Guatemala some of the densest and steepest jungle in the world. Added to which it is full of the most ferocious wildlife from alligators in the many rivers that the patrols must wade through, to extremely poisonous snakes. Soldiers spend a good deal of their time soaked to the skin because of the rainfall which can reach a phenomenal total of 170 inches a year, or soaked from their sweat with temperatures in their 100s accompanied by very high humidity. For the men on operational patrol ten days of compo rations, billy-can tea and mosquitoes in these conditions is usually quite enough.

Belize was founded as a British colony in 1662 although British settlers weren't allowed to move there until the late seventeenth century. It was then called British Honduras and since the early days there has been permanent hostility from the Guatemalans who have long been unsuccessfully demanding free access to the Caribbean through Belize.

In the 1970s there were three crises provoked by 'Guat' (as the troops call them) aspirations, and each time the British forces have responded with astonishing speed. British reinforcements were poured into this tiny country — smaller than Belgium — and with a population of only 120,000 citizens. The British acted with particular effect in the last crisis in 1977 when the force was doubled overnight with the addition of six vertical take-off Harrier Jump Jets as well as nearly two battalions of infantry with armour and artillery support. In 1978 there were still 2,000 servicemen remaining, 1,500 of them soldiers.

Since then the British have maintained a constant readiness for a Guatemalan invasion with the current force continually training in defensive measures. This force, in early 1984, included an armoured reconnaissance troop, a field artillery battery, an air defence detachment, one engineer squadron, one infantry battalion and one Army Air Corps detachment. Added to this there are several Harriers, Puma helicopters and half an RAF Regiment guarding ground installations with surface-to-air Rapier missiles.

The Army is mainly divided between north and south — in the north a battalion guards the area around Belize City and the flat open country that runs up to the northern border with Guatemala. In the south two companies regularly patrol in the extraordinarily dense jungle near the border, the other side of which are the natural harbours around Punto Gorda — much coveted by the Guatemalans.

Two main roads, one of them the Western highway, would be the main invasion route for Guatemalans but this would quickly be made impassable by the RAF Harriers able to attack any

WHERE ARE THEY NOW?
WO2 Mechen, Royal Marines

Life does not stand still in a working regiment. Civilians remember the Falklands campaign in terms of the media's coverage, a series of dramas frozen in time. The soldier's life carries on, and although the Falklands cannot fade away, with its harsh investment of blood and lives, the survivors have to get on with their job. The reality of service life is here and now, and while both soldier and civilian reminisce about past campaigns, the solider also has to live in the present.

For George Mechen, who as Company Sergeant Major of Yankee Company, 45 Commando, yomped from San Carlos to the battlefield of Two Sisters in the Falklands winter of June 1982, reality is the imminence of retirement from the Royal Marines. He deals with his war in a few brisk sentences: "We did the attacks on the night of the 11th and 12th of June. Then we did the surrender of Stanley. We stayed a while, cleaned the place up, got rid of the prisoners back to Argentina, then waited around for a ride home." Home is Arbroath, code name Condor, the base of the Marines' Mountain and Arctic Warfare Cadre. Home is also a little cottage in the hills near Arbroath, where he spent combined Easter, Summer and Falkland leave before returning to the rigorous cycle of Marine training.

"We launched ourselves straight into the remainder of the year's programme: mountain training at Glencoe. Basically it's the art of mountain warfare. That's what 45 Commando exists for: mountain and arctic warfare. Because we'd just spent a long time 'down there' (the Falklands), in the snow and the mountains, we half expected that the training might be overlooked, but no chance. We came back from leave and went straight to Glencoe. We do a month there at a time. When we'd done that we prepared for Norway, though at some stage the bodies of the guys who were killed came back by ship, and were released to the regiment. We buried all of them. Lots are buried actually in Arbroath cemetery, and lots are buried in their home towns. I took 'Y' Company down to Derby to bury Marine Novak. We gave him a large ceremonial funeral down there." 'Blue' Novak had been killed by machine-gun fire during Yankee Company's attack on Argentine positions at Two Sisters.

"After Christmas leave we went off in January, 1983, to Norway, for Arctic warfare training. We go there every year for three months. It's based in various Company locations. This time we lived in a very nice Norwegian holiday camp — like Butlins — in Trollhogda, which is just north of Narvik. That was our company base. The training involved a lot of company exercises, 1500 men at one time, all in the mountains there in Norway. Living in camp we enjoyed the good Norwegian food, but when we were out on exercise we went onto special Arctic rations. Unlike a normal ration pack, which is mainly tins, a ration pack for the Arctic is all dehydrated stuff. This is food for a watery environment. There's no shortage of water to mix it with in the snow. It's good value — lots of proteins and vitamins and anti-cold stuff." When 45 Commando was 'down south' in the Falkland campaign they were literally in their element, fighting in conditions and with equipment that the years of Arctic training had fitted them for ideally.

"Super keen and super-fit"

"Doing three months in Norway, practising arctic warfare, on skis — that really is the cherry on the cake for us once a year. We have a great time. The young guys learn to ski — in fact all 1500 learn to ski. Out on exercise we live for three weeks at a time out of base camp. We came back in early April, sailing from Norway in the *Hermes*. We anchored off Arbroath and were ferried off by helicopter straight to Condor airfield. They were Sea Kings, carrying about twenty-four men at a time."

As training routines continued, WO2 Mechen noticed a marked difference in the Falkland veterans. "The marines were super-keen and super-fit after doing time in the Falklands. For me the great bonus was to see that these quite young guys were a lot bigger mentally. I had dragged them all down there to the war and back again. Since then I've been on mountain training and to Norway with them several times, and I noticed a hell of a lot of changes, especially in Norway. They would take things in their stride that prior to the war they might have had reservations about. Especially up in the high mountains, in bad conditions. They coped. No bother at all. Just a few months earlier they'd been doing it for real. The guys were definitely twice as big mentally. It was great to watch them."

After three years as Company Sergeant Major of Y Company, George Mechen moved over to an administration job. He had been to Norway three times in that period, to Belfast, and to the Far East for jungle training, which was interrupted by the Falklands war. Since the Falklands the company has also been to Denmark and then France, training with the marine corps of those countries. Having moved over to 'give someone else a chance', he sees his new job as "a rest after three years of climbing mountains, digging holes, and eating bloody arctic ration packs." He keeps a company photograph in his new office, together with a collection of maps, photographs and other memorabilia of the Falklands war. He is aware that in some ways he stimulates the daily memories that keep cropping up by having all these reminders around him. "I'm trying to find the right way of saying this. The subject — the enormity of the whole bloody business — crops up in my brain every day. Every single day there are so many things that will remind you — the weather, or a face you recognise, or a map on the wall, or a picture, or whatever."

Marine uniform to give way to game-keepers plus-fours

WO2 Mechen is leaving the Royal Marines in February 1985, with 23 years service behind him. He will be 39 years old. And what will replace the hard physical existence of the marine, living out in wild country in all weathers? He is going to be a game-keeper. The cottage where he lives with his wife 10 miles from camp is the game-keeper's house for a large estate and shoot. His new charges will include pheasants, partridges and roe deer. Increasing deafness, the result of close exposure to explosions in Belfast, on training, and in the Falklands, has now virtually barred him from the type of soldiering he thrives on, the exercises, the mountain and warfare training, the range practice. And with it he misses the sense of belonging that seems stronger in highly trained units than anywhere else in the services. "I miss the whole saga of being the CSM of a rifle company, because its a great big machine, and it's great to be a key figure in it." WO2 Mechen has tried to convey the authentic experience of a marine in the slide-show lecturers he has given to civilian audiences since the Falkland war. As he says, "The story they want is the way it really happened, from ground level, and not the way they read it in the newspapers or in a book."

Yet in the final reckoning it may be impossible to convey what it is really like to have survived a war like that fought in the Falklands to someone who was not there.

"I still keep in contact with Y Company, though lots have gone on draft to other places. They'll come in and sit down, and have a natter. And really, this has happened a few times, you'll sit down, and look at each other, and you don't have to speak. You burst out laughing, or whatever, and you know just what each other's thinking — you're lucky to be alive, and lucky to be here, and, Jesus Christ . . . It's a hell of a thing."

Belize: hot, humid and full of nasty surprises for the unwary, it provides excellent jungle warfare training.

Belize: Cadenas observation point on the Guatemalan border, where troops watch the other side's activities.

approaching convoys. In the south, the jungles around Blue Creek Mountain are notoriously difficult to get through although British patrols are regularly sent out and even in this unlikely terrain there is a constant alert for possible invasion. Many of the mahogany and palm trees in the jungle grow to 100 feet in height cutting out the light and leaving behind them a tight undergrowth of shrubbery thick with large unpleasant spiders and tangles of roots. The worst offending wildlife that soldiers have to contend with are the coral and fer de lance snakes — the latter growing up to eight feet long and usually biting with fatal consequences. There are also tarantula spiders the size of saucers, and beef-bugs that burrow beneath the skin and grow the size of a finger. Soldiers using their machetes to clear a path through the undergrowth have to watch out also for the trees that, if struck, spurt a blistering acidic sap. Finally, there are the pumas and jaguars that no self-

respecting jungle would be without. To cope with these natural obstacles at least four men in every patrol have to be medically qualified and all section leaders carry morphine.

The Guatemalan border in the south does not relate to any natural geographical features; it is a straight line drawn through the jungle and patrolling it is doubtless as difficult for the Guatemalans as it is for the British.

Beneath the mountain peak of Cadenas in the south is the main Guatemalan outpost on the border and from a dug-in observation post on the British side, soldiers keep round-the-clock watch on activities far below. The Guatemalans would have difficulty reaching the OP, as do the British whose only means of getting there is by helicopter, a lifeline bringing in regular supplies. When it lands on a small, specially cleared piece of ground near the OP, the pilot keeps the blades rotating as fresh troops and

equipment are disembarked — to switch off would make the helicopter vulnerable to the high winds. Consequently troops and equipment come in with a swirl of debris.

Because Belize City is susceptible to flooding and was almost devastated in a bad flood in the early 60s, a new capital has been built in the centre of the country. Belmoplan sits in a low flat area south of the former capital and it is here that the British governor lives a secluded life in a bungalow surrounded by other government buildings and an indifferent central market place. Further north the main British base is Airport Camp near the immodestly named Belize International Airport — which is the only runway capable of landing jet aircraft, on one strip of tarmac. The RAF's detachment of Harriers are based here and these are guarded part of the time by a zealous locally-recruited force of 80 citizens called the Belize Defence Force.

Six miles away Belize City is hardly a high spot for the troops during leisure and spare time. Bisected by open sewers, the former capital is a conglomeration of festering wooden shanties with little in the way of amusement to offer the troops. The richer Belize citizens live in handsome residencies on the Atlantic coast and keep largely to themselves so most of the time soldiers and airmen keep to the NAAFI when they're not on duty. It is not surprising that to the few soldiers who get a tour in Belize, the country is known as the 'Hell-hole of Empire'. The chief reprieving factor is that the threat to Belize has to be taken seriously and visiting British servicemen are put on their metal. The south, in particular, offers an extremely good grounding in jungle warfare techniques.

Training in Brunei

Brunei is a tiny oil-rich sultanate on the north-east tip of Borneo. There is now only a garrison containing one Gurkha battalion and this may not be there much longer. There's also an Army Air Corps flight used for airlifting the visiting soldiers and Royal Marines who regularly go there for training. Brunei ceased to be a protectorate in 1959 but Britain retained responsibility for its defence — a responsibility from which the British have been trying to disengage for a number of years. There are still British officers and senior NCOs seconded to the Royal Brunei Malay Regiment which is the Sultan's own army, but the main purpose of Brunei to the British is for training in jungle warfare. It's like Belize but without any chance of hostility. Training is usually only conducted at about company level because facilities are limited. But this makes it ideal for giving crack British forces such as the Royal Marines Commandos four-weeks of intensive jungle experience.

Whether the Gurkha garrison stays is a subject of some contention; the Sultan wants them to remain while the British government see them as an easy target for defence budget pruning.

NATO's Southern Flank — Gibraltar and Cyprus

During the Second World War there were as many as 16,800 troops on Gibraltar — a tiny outcrop of British-owned rock occupying a very useful strategic position at the portals of the Mediterranean. The Army strength is now down to about 1,000 men including an infantry battalion, a surveillance troop and a specialist team of Royal Engineers all of whom get the backing of a detachment of Royal Artillery. For the Royal Navy, Gibraltar has long had an important significance; it is the base of the Navy's Mediterranean fleet and has a sizeable naval dockyard where refits can be undertaken. One frigate is permanently stationed there as well as a flight of Lynx helicopters. Finally, the RAF has a detachment of Jaguars which guards the airspace of the western Mediterranean.

Unfortunately, Gibraltar is not quite as attractive for British servicemen as it is sometimes made out to be. The night life is interesting certainly, and a great improvement on places like Brunei and Belize but the isthmuth is only two and a half square miles — which often gives troops stationed there a caged-in feeling. Recently the border with Spain has reopened after more than ten years so trips to La Linea are possible without having to go to Tangiers and back to Algeciras to get there.

But for military purposes Gibraltar is a natural fortress and houses about 20 miles of cool damp tunnels which can be put to a variety of uses in a wartime emergency. At present there's an electronic firing range secreted in this complex of tunnels which is used by all Services for range practice. Outside a newly built 'ruined village' offers troops a training ground for urban warfare tactics which is useful pre-Northern Ireland training. But the size of The Rock prevents the possibility of serious full-time land training so each battalion has to return to England for one or two months each year in order to keep up to scratch in battle fitness and fieldcraft.

Gibraltar's military accommodation is not everything it could be especially for single men. And this is another area where MOD financial provision is lacking as the British government is wary of providing expensive new housing units when the future of the garrison is somewhat in the balance. The Spanish have continually demanded the return of what they consider to be their property — and it was tension between these governments that resulted in the closing of the border. But since the death of General Franco and the restoration of a Spanish democratic government there has been increasingly less reason for the British to keep this isolated promontory — the more so since the Spanish joined the EEC. Gibraltarians, however, are extremely keen to remain in the British camp. Meanwhile relaxing servicemen make what they can of it and try to find a space on the crowded beaches.

Cyprus, secure and strategically important
Cyprus, on the other hand, is likely to stay 'British'

WHERE ARE THEY NOW?
Private Ian Davis
2 Para

Private Ian Davis has if anything become more determined since we spoke to him a year after the Falklands war had left him with a severely injured left arm and shoulder. At that time the arm was due for amputation, and he would have been invalided out of the 2nd Battalion of the Parachute Regiment as a matter of course. A year later he still has the arm, and is still in the regiment. But now Ian Davis wishes that they would amputate the arm. He foresees years of prolonged and probably fruitless surgery standing between him and his strongest ambition, which is, simply, to get on with his life.

"The surgeon has done something that very rarely works, an arthrodesis. It's the fusing of two bits of bone together, fastening what's left of the arm to what's left of the shoulder, so it doesn't move: you haven't got the joint there." His shoulder and arm were pinned together, and held with compression clamps, while the whole of his upper body was encased in plaster. There followed a series of infections. Sinuses formed in the damaged tissue, discharging infected material, and eventually osteomyelitis developed in the bone. So far this is confined to the upper arm, but Private Davis lives in constant discomfort. There is burning in the nerves, the limb and hand sweat a lot, and if he tries to grip anything he usually drops it.

Ian Davis is due to leave the army in 1985 when he will have completed his nine year engagement. Despite his shattered arm he is prepared to try and extend his service, but not at any cost. "I've been asking about staying in, but if they're just going to say 'You can only go up one rank', then it's pointless. I'd sooner go into civvy street. If they'd let me go up as far as sergeant eventually, then it would be worth it. But not just as a lance corporal." His fear is that, as a disabled soldier, he would be given some dead-end job in which to doze away his years. That is not Ian Davis's style, yet civilian life too is fraught with uncertainty. He has calculated that his disability pension and war pension together would total just over £40 a week tax free. The possibilities of receiving a lump sum from the Army Compensation Board are unclear. Information seems hard to come by. He has heard stories of some who have received large amounts, while others, with crippling disabilities, have been given relatively puny amounts. With all the options unresolved, Ian Davis considers it a 'Catch 22 situation' to be asked by the authorities whether he wants to stay in the army or get out. If he stays in, will he get reasonable prospects or a dead end? If he leaves, will he receive reasonable compensation for his disability, or a pittance?

Surgery interrupted computer course
If he had a job to go to, Private Davis says that he would leave the army. But with no job to go to, and no possibility of further operations on his arm for at least a year, he thinks it better maybe to bide his time, while trying to improve his qualifications. He

for a long while yet. A British colony for 35 years, Cyprus became independent in 1960 but Britain retained the two bases in the south — the Sovereign Base Areas (SBSs). In south-east there's Dhekelia and in the south-west, Akrotiri near the huge RAF airfield at Episkopi. The SBSs together take up 99 square miles of the island and are separated by 70 miles.

Like Gibraltar and Hong Kong, there has been some financial massaging in evidence in Cyprus with the once busy airport now only open for a few hours each day. Many squadrons have been removed. There are mainly soldiers left making up the armoured reconnaissance squadron, the engineer support squadron, one and a half infantry battalions and an Army Air Corps flight. The RAF have Phantom, Chinook, Buccaneer and Wessex detachments and one RAF Regiment guarding the garrison areas. And doing a very different job of keeping the peace between the Greeks and the Turks on the island since the Turkish invasion in

1974, Britain supplies nearly 800 soldiers to the United Nations Force in Cyprus — UNIFCYP. These troops spread along the buffer zone are usually on a six-months operational tour which is unaccompanied. Their compatriots further south are accompanied and wives and children make up a sizeable proportion of the British total. British UNIFCYP forces are deployed quite comfortably in what's called Section One to the west of Nicosia. The only dependents allowed here are those attached to the few officers and NCOs who take up staff appointments. The MOD has tried to ensure that the battalions on duty with UNIFCYP change round every six months so that each battalion gets an equitable share of the Cyprus sun. The changeover point is thus fixed for May and November each year.

Generally servicemen in Cyprus can enjoy the good beaches and fresh fruit of Cyprus but since 1974 the good tourist spots like Famagusta and Kyrenia have been closed off to them. But the Army lifestyle in Cyprus is on the whole a good one, with comfortable well-appointed bases which are guarded without too much military effort. Also in the south the British have access to the Cypriot Mount Olympus where a long range radar station has been set up and is strategically important for the eastern Mediterranean and Middle East.

Whilst the British have maintained an easy kind of independence in Cyprus, the Turks have demanded that we relinquish the Dhekelia SBA (where the main infantry battalion is housed — the two companies are based at Akrotiri) in return for the promise that they will let the Greeks settle in the area. But the British have no intentions of doing this. Cyprus is too good a strategic vantage point in the eastern Mediterranean. It is also a vital air-bridge for logistics and supply support to the UN peace-keeping forces based in the Lebanon and in Sinai. The logistics units in the two SBAs have this extra task.

Exercising abroad

Although British servicemen are not stationed in so many places abroad as used to be the case, many soldiers and airmen will get short-stay opportunities to visit foreign countries and train either in areas provided by the host countries or alongside troops from these countries. And British soldiers are increasingly undertaking joint training on the basis that this is good PR and shows willing. A recent Royal Marines Commando exercise, for example, in 1983 involved an eight-month voyage on HMS *Hermes*. The exercise was named Display Determination and was designed to show that NATO could readily reinforce and defend its Southern Flank; the Royal Marines disembarked and trained in Alexandria with the Egyptian army and invaded the shores of Turkey in a demonstration of amphibious speed and beach-head versatility.

---

and a friend from 3 Para, who also lost an arm in the Falklands, set out to learn computer programming. One of the first things Ian Davis had done back in England was to buy a computer, with a possible future career in programming in mind. Unfortunately classes were interrupted by the need for further medical treatment. Another possibility in which he is interested is the civil service. Deciding to bypass the bureaucracies, his wife wrote to Margaret Thatcher, explaining the circumstances, and enquiring what possibilities existed for Ian in the civil service. The reply referred him to the main recruiting centre, which sent on details about the diplomatic service. He has already taken an Executive Officer's test, but realises that his chances would be improved if he learned a foreign language, or managed to acquire computer experience.

Private Davis and his wife still live in married quarters in Aldershot, to which he is strongly attached because of the fellow feeling that exists between members of his regiment, especially those who were in the Falklands. With the help of the South Atlantic Fund he has bought a specially adapted Volvo which gives him a measure of independence. What he craves more than anything else is certainty. For that reason he would rather have no arm than a damaged one which might or might not get better. He would like a straight answer about his army prospects. Leave or stay, he needs a clear course of action. When he has one he will take it. He is currently trying to contact an American doctor who is developing a revolutionary new method of bone replacement surgery. Private Davis is impatient to get on with his life.

Above: A Royal Artillery 105mm Light Gun, fitted with skis, is prepared for firing during manoeuvres in northern Norway. Left: Men of 2 Para during exercise Trumpet Dance at Fort Lewis, Seattle, USA in February 1984. This involved a large scale stream descent from massive C141 Starlifter jet transport aircraft of the US Air Force.

Also in 1983 under the auspices of the Five Power Defence Arrangement, frigates that regularly patrol the Indian Ocean joined naval forces from Australia, Malaysia, New Zealand and Singapore in an exercise called Starfish which took place in the South China Sea. In the same year troops from the Hong Kong garrison went to Australia to do land training with Australian forces.

For obvious reasons it is the Royal Navy that sees the greatest part of the globe. In 1983 a group of seven naval warships headed by HMS *Invincible* deployed to the Caribbean where it exercised with the US and other friendly navies as well as doing weapon training and making a number of friendly visits. On each visit of a Royal Navy ship it is customary to 'show the flag' with local dignitaries being invited aboard and entertained by the officers in the wardroom. In this way the Navy has very much an ancillary ambassadorial role for the British.

The Army also have their share of regular visits. The Royal Armoured Corps, for example, trains for a number of weeks each year in the enormous Suffield range in Canada. The Royal Artillery and Infantry also train here and the three teeth arm forces link up to conduct exercises at battle group level. Whereas it takes a Chieftain tank only 45 minutes to get around the battle run at Hohne in Germany, it takes the same tank nearly four days on the Suffield range. The British make the most of this opportunity, for the few weeks they are there the British soldiers live in field conditions and are submitted to a hard daily round of activity until they leave.

Apart from Canada, in 1983 the Army trained in Singapore, Fiji, the USA (where two battalion-level exercises took place and the RAF did low-level

tactical training in Buccaneers, Jaguars and Hercules) Kenya (with two battalion and three company-level exercises and a Royal Engineer company training in construction and survey work), Malaysia, New Zealand and even doing one minor unit exercise in the Sudan.

And like Canada, Norway has become a regular training ground mainly for the Royal Marines. Commandos 42 and 45 are dedicated to Mountain and Arctic Warfare training which means extensive initial exercises in the rain and snow of Scottish highlands in winter, before embarking with full pack up to Norway for nearly three months at the beginning of each year until the thaw. The Royal Marines play a vital part in defending the NATO Northern Flank, often training alongside the Dutch marines who share this task. Their strategy is to hold any advancing Russian armour for as long as possible and practice skirmishing tactics similar to those employed by the Finns against the Russians in 1940. They train in cross-country skiing — ski-cross — in

Marines in northern Norway during a NATO exercise to reinforce the northern flank against possible incursion by Warsaw Pact armoured columns. The work is shared between British and Dutch marines, both seen here. 45 and 42 Commando, RM, are specialists in Mountain and Arctic warfare — training which came in unexpectedly useful during the Falklands campaign.

areas where the snow is too deep to go on foot and use the snow as a source of water as well as camouflage. Existing on an arctic ration pack containing a mere 5,000 calories a day, their worst enemy is the freezing temperatures that can reach as low as minus 45 degrees centigrade. They also learn to 'ski-jor' which is a more leisurely means of being towed behind the heavy tracked Volvo snow vehicles in small units for faster mobility.

The British Loan Service

The British forces have established an exceptionally good reputation abroad and the best proof of this is the fact that as many as 700 military personnel are

WHERE ARE THEY NOW?
Sgt Michael Kelly 2 Para

Sgt Michael Kelly has done 10 years in the regiment and has 12 to go. When the Falklands War broke out he was about to embark for Belize for jungle warfare training. After the Falklands, he took his leave, and then proceeded with cadre training. Every year or 18 months NCOs carry out cadre training in specialist platoons, concentrating on one specific field skill such as anti-tank operations, or signals. Sgt Kelly welcomed the parachute jumping included in his cadre training, as he had not jumped for almost nine months, due largely to the Falklands campaign. When the period of training was over, he went out with most of the 2nd Battalion to do the (forestalled) Belize tour.

Belize is a six month tour that provides the best available jungle warfare training for British troops. HQ was at an airport just outside Belize city, and Sgt Kelly was involved with administration as well as exercises and adventure training. Tour duties included jungle patrolling, OPs — spending time at observation posts looking out over the border into Guatemala, and base camp duties such as fatigues. Belize provides experience of what is known as 'dirty' jungle. Diseases and unpleasant animal life such as insects and snakes are rife. The jungle is always wet. You patrol all day in wet clothing, change into dry gear for the night, and then put the wet stuff back on again in the morning. Jungle gear consists of lightweight clothing made of camouflage DPM (Disruptive Pattern Material), together with jungle boots and webbing, plus the ever present Bergen rucksack. Patrols go from one of the 4 location areas out to a patrol base for a 7 to 10 day stint. They go out from this base for one or two days at a time, up to thirty strong, carrying food and water with them. They always sleep in hammocks, never on the ground. Ponchos help to keep off rain, and mosquito nets are essential, though despite these, and a daily ration of Paludrin tablets, a couple of the paratroopers still developed malaria back in the UK after the Belize tour. The jobs carried out by the patrols include the cutting of helicopter landing sites in the jungle, and the checking out of previously cut sites to see if they have become overgrown.

Rest and recreation (R&R) can be taken wide afield from Belize, and paratroopers travelled to Mexico and the US, though some, like Sgt Kelly, stayed put. He travelled no further than St George's Quay, an army training camp on an island off Belize, for a course in scuba diving. Some members of the Battalion travelled to Fort Bragg in Texas, where they exercised with US paratroopers in order to win their US Airborne Paratroop wings.

Sgt Kelly returned to the UK in the first week of October, 1983, for more parachute jumping, and courses in free-falling. Paratroopers from 2 Para spent two stints of 4 or 5 days at Greenham Common when the US missiles were being brought in, and then went on Xmas leave.

Straight after Xmas the Battalion took part in a short three to four day exercise coming under the heading of 5 Airborne Brigade, Out of Area Operations. This emphasized a new 'go anywhere' role, and is specifically not committed to NATO. UK exercises took place with different scenarios, and included mass drops of brigade (400) strength, together with equipment and transport drops.

Trumpet Dance

At the beginning of February 2 Para continued Out of Area Operations training on an even larger scale. The whole active Battalion flew out in Tristars from the UK to Fort Lewis, Seattle, in the state of Washington, USA. There they were billeted in a vast complex of two-storey blocks. Fort Lewis was like nothing the paras had ever seen before, an army base as big as a city, with numerous shops, eating places and theatres as well as the more familiar military architecture. The five-week spell at Fort Lewis began with range practice, and then continued with live ammunition exercises at the Yakima Firing Center in the Cascade Mountains where the British soldiers spent ten days in a training area of wild country some six times the size of their familiar Brecon Beacons. A further three days and nights were spent at the US Army's Winter Training School at Huckleberry Creek, and in a further three-day exercise the Paras were ferried by helicopter into forested country to rescue 'hostages' held captive by 'terrorists'.

The culmination of the mass exercise, code-name 'Trumpet Dance', was a large scale stream descent of 607 parachutists, consisting of 507 Paras plus 100 men of the US 2nd Battalion of the 75th Rangers. Eight C141 B Starlifter jets carried the parachutists. Those who made the drop — and that includes every qualified man in 2 Para — found the experience exhilarating, not least the sensation of 'walking' out of the C141s, rather than jumping out in the familiar Hercules style.

Back in the UK Company and Brigade level exercises, with up to 120 men in a Company group, continued with a parachute force of an estimated 1800 taking part. All in all, 2 Para had been in their Aldershot barracks only 2 months of the last 12.

Marine in snow camouflage shoulders Blowpipe anti-tank weapon system.

Scimitar armoured reconnaissance vehicles in snow camouflage during manoeuvres in Norway. With the rapid-fire 30mm Rarden gun, Scimitar is a formidable light tank.

sent to various countries to train newly evolving armed forces, or to help out Commonwealth countries in beleaguered circumstances.

Oman in the '70s was a clear demonstration of the extraordinary efficacy of only a few British servicemen in helping the Sultan to put down a rebellion of guerrillas in the Dhofar province. Until quite recently about 60 SAS troops remained to train the local *Firkat* force in counter-insurgency techniques. But normally the military tasks require a smaller force. One example of a current deployment of officers and NCOs is to Lesotho where three British officers from different regiments has been endeavouring, since 1982, to get the keen Lesotho soldiers into a well-disciplined fighting force run broadly on British lines. The problem is that every soldier wants to be a warrior and it has been hard to impress the Lesotho force that support in the form of well organised administration is as vital as a well trained front line. At their disposal the training team

have a pot-pourri of weapons including 81mm mortars, American 106mm anti-tank guns mounted on Iranian jeeps, a 20mm Oerlikon wheeled anti-aircraft gun, as well as MAN and Leyland trucks and Shorland armoured personnel carriers. British officers in this position have to rely on their instincts and invention to make a streamlined and coherent force with such equipment.

Such problems are typical of the loan service personnel operating, as they invariably do, in the underdeveloped countries.

All things considered, British military enterprise is much more of a global affair than other western industrial countries with the certain exception of the USA. But there are many question marks hanging over the future of many of the former training grounds of empire and as each colony or dependency is given up, greater input has tended to be put into establishing informal training links with other countries. Whilst the single largest problem is the availability of funds, the Falklands experience has proved that whatever the terrain or the conditions, the military experience will be there to meet the challenge.

Chapter 7

NEW EQUIPMENT: THE FORCES RE-ARM

A large part of Britain's conventional armoury has now been combat tested for the first time, and all three Forces are re-equipping with new or modified weaponry and hardware to replace losses and to make up for existing stock found wanting or outdated.

RFA helicopter training ship, *Contender Bezant*, being fitted out at Harland and Wolff. She will replace *Engadine*.

EQUIPPING THE NAVY: MICROCHIPS AND MISSILES

The sinking of four modern British warships in the Falklands raised many doubts about their design and equipment. In particular the sinking of the destroyer *Coventry* raised doubts about the efficiency of her Seadart missiles and surveillance radars. There was also considerable criticism from the frigates in San Carlos Water about the difficulty of detecting targets approaching over land.

The bitter truth is that in 1982 the Royal Navy was still largely equipped with radars designed 30 years earlier. The Type 965, despite small improvements, was an elderly radar intended only to detect bombers at medium altitude. It has a slow data-rate, making it unsuitable for tracking fast, low-level targets, and was in addition difficult to maintain. Its faults had been recognised, but the replacement, designated Type 1030, had been cancelled in 1980 in a series of defence cuts demanded by Mr (later Sir) John Nott. An interim set, however, had been designed. Called Type 1022, it used Dutch processing with British antenna. This radar was fitted in several destroyers, and the carrier *Invincible*, and operators reported that it was a great improvement.

The Seadart missile system relies on the Type 965 or Type 1022 radar to locate targets at maximum range, after which individual targets are designated by a Type 992 radar. This radar proved very poor at distinguishing low-flying targets over land as it has never received the necessary improvements to do so. This imposed a severe handicap in air defence around San Carlos Water, but in spite of this the Type 909 missile trackers obtained some remarkable results, and there is ample evidence that the Argentine pilots had a healthy respect for the Seadart's capabilities. The main weakness was the need for a manual transfer of data from the air warning (965 or 1022) radar to the trackers; a simple human error under stress could result in an invalid firing. The destructive effect of guided missiles had been known for a long time; the battleship *Warspite* had been crippled by German glider-bombs as long ago as 1943 and the sinking of the Israeli destroyer *Eilat* in 1967 had caused a 'missile panic' among the world's navies. Ironically this 'panic' produced the French Exocet anti-ship missile, and the Royal Navy became the first customer for it in 1970.

The standard means of defence against sea-skimming missiles like Exocet is to detect the transmissions of the radar seeker in the guidance system,

Sea Dart missile leaves its launcher on a RN Type 82 destroyer. Sea Dart is a third generation area defence system against low level air attack.

and then to fire clouds of 'chaff', metallic strips cut to the right length to produce a false radar-echo. Clouds of chaff, thrown into the air by rockets, fall slowly like autumn leaves, creating a false image in the missile's 'brain'. HMS *Sheffield* was equipped with the standard chaff-launchers and missile-detecting gear, but because the electronic support measures (ESM) or signal-detection equipment was inexplicably left switched off she had no warning of the approaching Exocet, until it was spotted visually — too late to do anything about it. Other Exocet attacks were, however, defeated by the same combination of ESM and chaff, so there was no doubt about the efficiency of the countermeasures when used correctly.

There are two additional weapons against sea-skimmers, active jamming of the guidance system or shooting the missile down with short-range guns, and both are valuable adjuncts to chaff and ESM. Unfortunately the Royal Navy, like the US Navy, had been sceptical about the value of jammers, believing that they 'beacon' or give away the position of the ship. That assertion is true up to a point, but once an Exocet has locked onto a target there is little point in worrying about giving that target's position away. Jamming is therefore an essential element in the defence against such attacks. The Royal Navy's plans to add an active jammer, to its existing ESM equipment, had been cancelled under the Nott cuts in 1981, but industry proved capable of filling the gap at short notice. The latest frigates are to receive new electronic warfare equipment.

The Royal Navy had been very sceptical about the value of guns against missiles, preferring to rely on the Seawolf missile, but the shock of events in May 1982 forced a rapid about-face. The US Navy was asked to make available sufficient Mk 15 Phalanx 20mm 'Gatling' guns to arm the carriers *Invincible* and *Illustrious* with two each (plus one mounting for training). A detailed evaluation of other systems started afterwards, and this year the choice was made in favour of the Dutch 30mm Goalkeeper system. Although the various systems work in different ways they have one thing in common: very high rates of fire, which direct streams of shells in the path of an incoming missile. Goalkeeper uses a rotary 30mm gun to fire thousands of tungsten-cored rounds, forming a 'wall of lead' through which the missile cannot fly without striking several projectiles. The missile's warhead is sufficiently delicate to be put out of action by such a bombardment, and it will either veer out of control or explode prematurely.

Above: A Wallop 'Barricade' Naval Decoy system which fires Chaff and infra red decoys as counter-measures to missile attack seen aboard a Navy Fast Patrol Boat.

Below, left: Mk 15 20mm Phalanx 'Gatling' guns are being fitted to *Invincible* and *Illustrious*. Below: Dutch-built close-in 30mm weapon system, Goalkeeper, firing.

Finding the space

The newer ships of the Royal Navy, such as the Type 22 frigates and the *Invincible* class carriers are easy to fit, but finding deck-space in older frigates and the Type 42 destroyers will be tricky. The Type 21 frigates and the Type 42 destroyers suffer very much from being designed to strict limits on dimensions and tonnage, and installing a bulky system such as Goalkeeper will tax the designers' ingenuity to the utmost.

The Royal Navy's faith in its Seawolf missile system was amply justified in spite of the fact that it did not engage Exocet. Its main drawback is that in its original form it is extremely heavy and bulky, ensuring that it could only be fitted in comparatively large frigates. As the Type 42 missile-armed destroyers were built to restricted dimensions they could not accommodate Seawolf, nor could the commercially-designed Type 21. The former were supposed to rely on the low-level performance of Seadart, and the latter did at least have Seacat, but neither system was ever intended to cope with multiple attacks.

Fortunately Seawolf has been under continuous development, first to reduce its weight and then to find a method of vertical launching. The great advantage of vertical launch is that every round is ready to fire, for each missile is housed in a canister counter-sunk into the deck or arranged on either side of deckhouses.

Even the cramped Type 42 destroyers can benefit from the improvements to Seawolf, and plans have been prepared to give them a much-needed upgrading. The major improvement would be the substitution of the after Type 909 Seadart tracker radar with two versions of a new Marconi radar, one dedicated to Seadart and the other to Seawolf. The advance of electronics since the 909 was designed 25 years ago is such that the weight of both trackers is less than one 909. The ships would also need a new surveillance radar, capable of designating targets to the Seadart system.

The radar problem has been tackled vigorously since 1982, proof of how urgent the Royal Navy felt the problem to be. But instead of specifying a complex and expensive radar to meet its requirements, the Navy put the proposal out to industry to see which commercial radar sets could come close to its requirements. To ensure that the radar chosen was adequate the competition used what is called Cardinal Point Specification. In other

Left: First vertical-launch test firing of Seawolf anti-missile missile. The advantage of vertical launch is to reduce cramping and increase payload on crowded decks. Right: Submarine-launched Harpoon missile breaks surface, its launch-canister head flying away. Harpoon is capable of being fired from standard, unmodified, torpedo tubes.

words, irreducible minimum standards were set for certain crucial areas, but outside those the manufacturer was free to follow his own commercial practice.

The contract for the new Type 996 radar went to Plessey last year. The radar is basically a derivative of two existing radars, the AWS-5 surveillance radar already sold to Denmark and Nigeria, and the AWS-6, a low-level radar developed for a Swiss anti-missile gun system. The AWS-6 is specifically designed to detect and track sea-skimming missiles, essential for both Seawolf and the Goalkeeper system. The new radar will go to sea in the new Type 23 frigates and will be retrofitted to the Type 42 destroyers and other ships.

To improve its striking power the Royal Navy is adopting an American anti-ship missile, the Harpoon. Proof that the lessons are being learned is the doubling of numbers, from four Exocets apiece in current warships to eight in new construction. Another sign of fresh thinking is the reinstatement of medium-calibre guns. Before the Falklands most naval opinion rejected the gun as virtually useless, a 'popgun' suitable only for law-enforcement in peacetime. During the 14 weeks of Operation Corporate the Mk 6 and Mk 8 guns of the Task Force fired over 8000 rounds, proving how wrong that opinion had been. The 4.5 inch Mk 8 gun has replaced a 3 inch

The Royal Navy's new stretched Type 22 Broadsword class destroyer, HMS *Boxer*, offers substantially greater weapons deck space than her predecessors, especially ones fitted out with vertical launch Seawolf.

gun planned for the Type 23, and the latest version of the Type 22 frigates have also had a 4.5 inch added to the design.

The war below the waves

In the world of anti-submarine warfare many of the problems were already in hand. The new Stingray torpedo, for example, has much better shallow-water performance than the Mk 46 used in 1982. Operators of the new Type 2016 sonar in the *Broadsword* and *Brilliant* reported very favourably on the equipment, and the nuclear submarines had the opportunity to try out their towed arrays in operational conditions. Like the gun, the old depth-charge mortars were regarded as obsolescent, but it was soon proved that the deterrent effect of a 'big bang' was considerable — a homing torpedo which misses usually makes no noise, and therefore contributes very little to the strain on the submarine commander.

Mines are among the most potent and cost-effective weapons in the naval inventory, and the Task Force went to the Falklands well prepared for Argentine efforts to mine Port Stanley. This was a wise precaution, for the new minehunters *Brecon* and *Ledbury* swept two minefields. Also tested was a new concept of wire sweeping for deep-laid mines, using five chartered trawlers. The mines found proved to be comparatively unsophisticated by today's standards, but the experience was invaluable.

Although four warships were sunk, surprisingly few weaknesses in basic design came to light. The *Sheffield* stayed afloat for days after being hit, while the *Antelope* was only destroyed when a bomb

Marconi's lightweight Stingray torpedo being deployed from a Royal Navy Sea King helicopter by parachute to reduce the danger of damage hitting the sea. Stingray is a high-speed 'intelligent' torpedo.

detonated in her Seacat magazine. *Coventry* and *Ardent* both succumbed to overwhelming air attack, and in all four ships loss of life was remarkably light. The quantity of inflammable materials in ships was rapidly reduced, and it has proved comparatively easy to divide ships into smoke-zones to improve firefighting. Sadly, it takes a war to convince people of the value of such measures, but once learned the lessons have proved relatively easy to put into practice.

NATO requirements limit Navy's role

The real problem for the Royal Navy revealed by the Falklands is not concerned directly with equipment and weapons. It is a NATO problem, for NATO does not encourage its member navies to think too deeply about 'out-of-theatre' operations. Successive British governments have played the NATO card, cutting back every year on any capability not demanded by NATO. This, as much as anything, accounted for the Royal Navy's lack of airborne early warning radar, and its lack of defences against air attack. As a mid-Atlantic escort force there would be no need for close range defence against aircraft, no need for amphibious warfare, and no need for long range. It was a self-fulfilling prophecy, as navies like the Dutch and British rid themselves of expensive aircraft carriers and turned themselves into single-mission forces.

NATO thinking is dominated by the Central Front and fears of a massive Warsaw Pact assault across the plains of Germany. But all evidence since 1945 points to lower-level conflict well away from Central Europe. All conflicts have taken place outside the NATO area, and even where the major powers have become involved the level of conflict has remained low, with no threat of a nuclear holocaust. The Gulf War between Iran and Iraq is only the latest of these, and the question must be asked, how is NATO to cope with such dangerous events?

Nations with no economic stake in the Gulf cannot

Further evidence of the effectiveness of long range anti-ship missiles: tanker ablaze in the Persian Gulf in 1984, an unfortunate victim of the escalating Iran-Iraq conflict and proof of the worldwide threat to shipping.

be expected to send ships to the area, but what does a maritime nation like Britain do when her shipping is threatened? She can in theory leave everything to the Americans, but for a variety of good diplomatic and political reasons she is bound to send warships, even if they join a multi-national force.

In today's violent world Exocet missiles may be fired at ships, whether they belong to a belligerent nation or not. A warship or a merchant ship could well be fired on off the Libyan coast, and in recent months tankers have been attacked off Kharg Island refinery in the Gulf. Given that risk, the single-role warship favoured by NATO navies is going to be at a great disadvantage. The truth is that the interests of individual NATO members often lie outside NATO, and if those interests can be defended by warships, then the navy concerned will have to build ships capable of operating further afield.

To sum up, the Falklands experience suggests that the next generation of Royal Navy warship needs better endurance, and sufficient offensive and defensive armament to operate in a hostile environment. This does not mean that cheap and cost-effective ships cannot be built for peace-time duties, but there must be an end to building deliberately second-class ships such as those built in the 1960s and early 1970s. All the economies are wiped out if the ship gets sunk easily. Until such time as a way is found of transporting large quantities of heavy military equipment without ships, there will be a need for warships to get the ships there safely.

EQUIPPING THE ARMY — 'BATTLE-LAB' RESULTS

For the Army, as much as the other two Services, the Falklands Campaign was a useful test laboratory for weapons systems and equipment. While training exercises and range firing can go a long way towards proving weapons and equipment, it is not until they are used in an active service environment, with all the attendant stresses, both physical and psychological, that they can be said to have undergone the ultimate test.

By 1982 it was almost thirty years since the British Army had been involved in a general war conflict, Korea. Although Suez in 1956 and the Radfan in the 1960s approached this, the former was over very quickly, while the latter was more akin to the old style Frontier skirmishes in India. As for the other campaigns — Malaya, Cyprus, Borneo, Aden and Northern Ireland — these have been counter-insurgency operations, requiring skills and weapons not wholly applicable to a general war context. In any event, there had been no opportunity to try out many weapons systems, either because they had only been recently introduced or because they were not suited to counter-insurgency operations. Thus, systems like the 105mm Light Gun, the Combat Vehicle Reconnaissance (Tracked) (CVR(T)) Scorpion and Scimitar, the Milan Anti-Tank Guided Weapon (ATGW) system, and the Rapier and Blowpipe air defence systems were receiving their baptism of fire.

Yet, although there was obviously much official interest in the way that weapons and equipment had performed in the Falklands and immediate extensive post-war analyses within the Ministry of Defence, it must be pointed out early on that the campaign was considered as a 'one off' and not a sign that British defence policy was switching its priority from NATO in Europe to out-of-area operations. The current role of the British Army remains directed firmly towards the NATO Central Region and the emphasis in weapons procurement still rests on the mobile armoured battle that is likely to be fought there, should a major war in Europe break out. The Falklands was very much an infantryman's war, and the harshness of the terrain very unlike the woods, hills and growing conurbisation of the Federal Republic of Germany. That said, however, the Falklands experience cannot be totally divorced from the British Army's roles today.

For a start, NATO is now realising that threats to the Alliance can come from outside Europe — Middle East oil on which its members are so dependent is a prime example. This is reflected in the setting up of the US Rapid Deployment Force and the French Force d'Action Rapide. These

Top: Scorpion (foreground) and Scimitar CVR(T) armoured vehicles on exercise in Norway, part of the multi-nation force protecting Nato's Northern Flank.
Above: The portable, 2-man operated Milan Anti-tank Guided Weapon System.

Alvis Samson Armoured Recovery Vehicle. On today's high-tech battlefield, Engineers need armour protection as much as other front-line troops.

require the ability to be moved quickly over long distances to counter a potential threat and, once deployed, must be capable of holding off more heavily equipped forces. The British response to this has been to convert 5 Infantry Brigade, which, of course, played an important part in the Falklands, into a more responsive force by giving it an airborne capability and redesignating it 5 Airborne Brigade. There is, too, Britain's contribution to the Allied Command Central Europe Mobile Force (Land) (AMF(L)). This is a quick deploy force designed to operate on the flanks of NATO — Scandinavia, Greece and Turkey — in the event of a Soviet threat to those regions, in order to deter aggression by demonstrating NATO solidarity. The British provide an infantry battalion, 105mm Light Gun battery, armoured reconnaissance squadron, communications and logistic assets to AMF(L). Furthermore, there is Britain's permanent contribution to NATO's northern flank in Norway in the shape of 3 Commando Brigade and 1 Infantry Brigade. These elements are expected to deploy, fight and sustain themselves in conditions comparable to those in the Falklands. Thus, the lessons drawn in terms of weapons and equipment used in the South Atlantic do have relevance.

In order to review the lessons learnt and implications for the future, it is easiest to consider each arm and service. In terms of seniority, armour comes first and this is represented by the two CVR(T) troops of the Blues & Royals (Royal Horse Guards/Dragoons). Each troop consisted of two Scorpions with a 76mm gun and two Scimitars with the 30mm Rarden gun. In addition, there was a CVR(T) Samson recovery vehicle to give the troops maintenance support. They were sent in the knowledge that the Argentinians had light armoured vehicles on the Falklands but, on arrival, with the Argentinian armour seemingly unwilling to venture outside Port Stanley, coupled with the belief that the boggy terrain would severely hamper their mobility, there was a certain amount of doubt as to whether they could play a useful role. This changed dramatically with the decision to switch them from the northern axis to support 5 Brigade in the south. They were allowed 24 hours to redeploy on the assumption that they would have to use tracks and none ran across the central hinterland. On their own initiative, they

Inside the Samson: using the same hull as the Alvis Spartan APC, Samson is equipped with a heavy-duty winch, anchoring spades, tools and recovery equipment.

struck off directly cross-country and completed the move in six hours. What this proved was the CVR(T)'s low nominal ground pressure, which is achieved by the use of aluminium armour, was more than sufficient to tackle the terrain. Once, with 5 Brigade, it was in the fire support role that they proved invaluable. The 76mm gun has two main types of round, High Explosive Squashhead (HESH) and an HE round, and the latter was used to great effect as a supplement to the artillery. The Rarden 30mm, with its burst fire capability, was also very useful in terms of suppressive fire. In addition, CVR(T)'s image intensification and thermal imaging devices meant that accurate fire could be put down by night as well as day, and also was a very good sur-veillance aid.

Anti-armour role needs to be established

Thus CVR(T) more than fulfilled its promise. There was, however, one area in which it was not tested and that was in the anti-armour role. Although its prime role is reconnaissance and British doctrine works on the principle that this should be by stealth, there are times when information will have to be fought for, which means engaging enemy armour. While both the 76mm and 30mm are known to be effective against light armour, they will not make much impression on main battle tanks, especially if engaged from the front. Yet, in the rapid deployment scenario, anti-armour rather than reconnaissance may well be their prime role, at least during the initial stages, when waiting for the sealift to reinforce airlift with heavier weapons systems. Alvis Ltd, who make CVR(T), have, however, developed Scorpion 90, armed with the Belgian Cockerill 90mm gun, and it may well be that this, with its increased anti-armour performance over the 76mm, can provide the answer to the dilemma.

Turning to artillery, the old adage that there is never enough artillery on the battlefield was amply reinforced by the Falklands. The 35 105mm Light Guns which the Task Force had were at times very stretched to fulfil all that was demanded of them. Indeed, at Goose Green, 2 Para were supported by three guns only, all that could be made available, and this made their task immeasurably more difficult. The Light Gun itself has now been in service with the British Army for some ten years, superseding the

The all-British 105mm Light Gun of the Royal Artillery being fired on Salisbury Plain. Its 35lb shell can reach up to 11 miles, and proved highly effective during Corporate.
Right: Para using the binocular-based Laserguide LP7 rangefinder.

Italian 105mm pack howitzer. It fires a 35lb shell to a range of over 10 miles, and, in spite of the problems of 'bedding in' on the very soft ground, proved to be remarkably accurate. One aspect which contributed especially to the effectiveness of the artillery was the fire control equipment used by forward observation parties, whose responsibility it is to acquire targets and direct fire onto them. This has been revolutionised by the laser target designator, which gives an accurate and precise range from the observer to the target. Although the gunners took their own designators and night vision equipment with them, it was too heavy to carry over the long 'yomps' and they made do with infantry night sights and hand-held laser designators, which worked extremely well. The need, however, to give forward observation parties lighter and more manageable equipment has resulted in developments in this field. Based on binoculars, the firm of Lasergage, whose LP7 rangefinder was

Shoulder-launched, man-portable, anti-armour weapon system Blowpipe proved too slow and insufficiently powerful against high-speed aircraft in the Falklands and is now being replaced.

used in the Falklands, has now produced a lighter version, which gives not just a range read-out, but a bearing observer-to-target as well, which is another vital piece of information needed by the guns in order to compute the correct lay. This rapidly speeds up the target acquisition time over the traditional method of using a field compass, and will result in the guns being even more responsive than before.

Another crucial role of the Royal Regiment of Artillery is air defence, and this too was, from the outset, vitally important in the campaign. Two air defence systems were used, Rapier and the hand-held Blowpipe. Initially the Rapier crews took time to adapt to active service conditions, but rapidly mastered them, and the system proved very effective against fast low flying aircraft, precisely the type of target for which it is designed. When first deployed, it was without the 'Blindfire' radar system, which enables it to operate in all weathers and by both day and night, and operators had to rely on optical tracking once the target had been spotted by the acquisition radar. Furthermore, the acquisition radar was on the same frequency as some of those used on the ships, which caused some interference. In addition, that used on the Falklands was the towed version, using a Land-Rover, and it took time to set

up. Indeed, part of the reason for the disaster at Fitzroy was because the Rapiers, although they had been landed, were not yet operational when the Argentinian aircraft made their attacks on *Sir Galahad* and *Sir Tristram*. The tracked version, which is now coming into service, can be made operational very much more quickly, and, certainly within the Central Region, will be a great improvement on the towed version.

Javelin to replace underpowered Blowpipe

If Rapier more than lived up to the hopes for it, Blowpipe was a disappointment. While it was effective enough against helicopters and slow flying fixed wing aircraft like the Pucará, it was no match for the high speed Mirages and Skyhawks. The problem was twofold. Firstly, the Blowpipe system is relatively heavy and cumbersome and the missile was simply not fast enough to catch the faster jets unless they were flying head-on. Indeed, the Special Air Service used the US General Dynamics Stinger

system and achieved much better results with it. Short Brothers of Belfast, who make Blowpipe, have, as a result of the lessons learnt, brought out Javelin, which is an advance variant of Blowpipe. It has a new and more lethal warhead and a more powerful second stage motor designed to extend its range. In addition, the guidance system is now Semi-Automatic Command to Line of Sight (SACLOS) instead of the Manual Command to Line of Sight (MACLOS) system used on its predecessor. This means that the operator, instead of having to simultaneously track the target and manually guide the missile along the line of sight, now merely has to maintain his aim on the target and the missile will automaticaly respond and fly along the line of sight. These improvements will make Javelin very much more effective than its predecessor.

The role of the engineers in war is to impede the

Left: Short Brothers' updated version of Blowpipe, Javelin, is faster, considerably more lethal in hitting power, and lighter than its predecessor.

RSAF Individual Weapon system

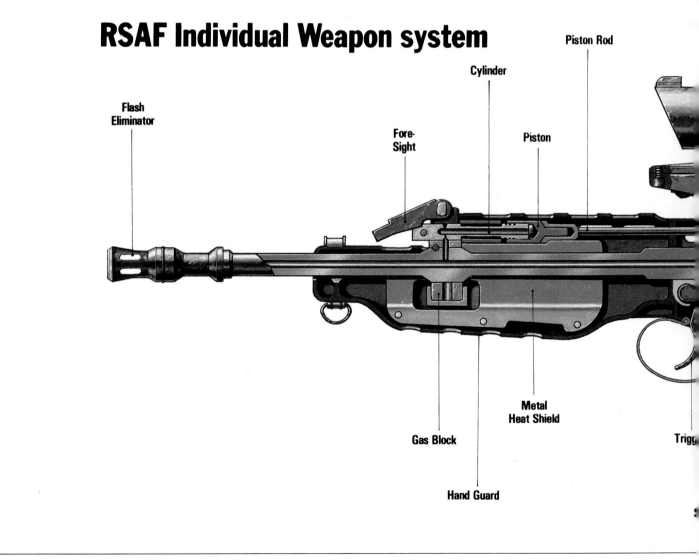

Flash Eliminator

Fore-Sight

Cylinder

Piston Rod

Piston

Gas Block

Metal Heat Shield

Hand Guard

Trigg

enemy's mobility while enhancing that of their own side. In the Falklands, because the British were advancing and the Argentinians defending, the Argentinian engineers were concerned with the first role and the British with the second. More than anything else this revolved around mines. The Argentinians made extensive use of minefields and a number of British casualties resulted, even after hostilities were over during the massive clearance operation that still continues in order to make the Islands safe once more for humans and animals. Initially, the British believed that the Argentinians possessed only obsolete Italian metallic mines, both anti-armour and anti-personnel. It was thus thought that the British Army's standard detector, the No 4C made by United Scientific Instruments Ltd and capable of detecting metallic mines only would be quite sufficient. In the event, it was discovered that

the Argentinians were using not just Italian mines, but ones produced by themselves, Israeli, American and Spanish types as well. What was more serious was that many of them were plastic and could not be located by the No 4C Detector. While the conflict raged and immediately after the armistice, the Royal Engineers were reduced to using the primitive probe, nothing more than a metal spike, for discovering mines, and this proved to be a ponderous and nerve-racking method of overcoming the problem. Consequently, non-metallic detectors had to be brought in from the United States, and since then, in view of increasing appearance of the plastic mine, United Scientific Instruments have now developed their NMD78 detector, which will work against both non-metallic and metallic mines. This is still being refined, but is likely to enter British Army service shortly.

The British Army's new Individual Weapon system is based on the RSAF's experimental 4.85mm assault rifle, subsequently recalibred to standard NATO 5.56mm.

7.62 vs 5.56

In terms of infantry weapons, the Self-Loading Rifle, which has now been in British Army service for well

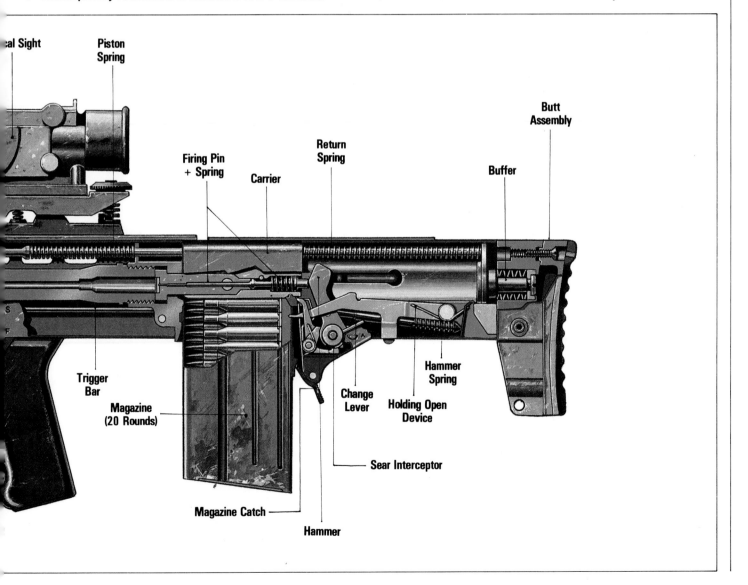

al Sight
Piston Spring
Firing Pin + Spring
Carrier
Return Spring
Butt Assembly
Buffer
Trigger Bar
Magazine (20 Rounds)
Change Lever
Holding Open Device
Hammer Spring
Sear Interceptor
Magazine Catch
Hammer

over twenty years, once again stood up well to conditions. Now, however, it is about to be replaced by the 5.56mm Personal Weapon, part of the SA-80 small arms family developed by the Royal Small Arms Factory, Enfield. What was particularly impressive was the stopping power of the 7.62mm round, which Special Forces members using the US M16 Armalite, which is also of 5.56mm calibre, very much missed. On the other hand, another old and tried lesson re-learnt was the vital importance of winning the firefight, which means that the infantryman must have the capability to put down an immediate and sustained concentration of fire in order to neutralise his enemy immediately prior to and during the assault. This means carrying a large quantity of ammunition, but the 7.62mm round is significantly heavier than the 5.56mm. He was thus limited on the Falklands as to what he could carry and, in order to carry more, was forced to discard other items of his equipment. This was even more of a problem with the 7.62mm General Purpose Machine Gun using belt ammunition and the Light Machine Gun with magazines, and machine gunners often ran out of ammunition very early on in the battle. The Light Support Weapon, the other member of the SA-80 family, which is designed to replace both in the dismounted role in the infantry section, will also reduce this problem. The GPMG in the sustained fire role, which is using a tripod rather than bipod, and the sniper's rifle, currently the L42A1, will, however, remain calibered 7.62mm because they need to be effective at ranges greater than that of 300m, the maximum effective range of SA-80, which was confirmed in the Falklands as being sufficient for the section battle.

Of the other weapons used at section level, the US M79 Grenade Launcher, which up until the Falklands had been used merely to fire CS gas and dye marker grenades against unruly crowds in Northern Ireland, was found to be very effective with its HE grenade in close quarter battle and, on the NATO scene, will be very useful in Fighting in Built-Up Areas (FIBUA), an area to which the British Army is now paying very much more attention than previously. The L2 hand grenade was also much used in flushing out machine gun nests hidden in the rocky outcrops. Likewise the US 66mm Light Anti-Armor Weapon (LAW), a one shot throwaway recoilless rocket system, was also useful when misemployed against sangars. Both this, and its big brother, the platoon level 84mm Carl Gustav, are to be replaced by LAW 80. This is nothing to do with the Falklands experience, but because the 94mm projectile of LAW 80 will be better able to deal with the ceramic type of armour found on the present generation of main battle tanks. The same applies to Milan ATGW. At the time, much was made in the media of the use of this weapon to blast away Argentinian strongpoints. This, however, was technically misusing it, and it had only been taken by 3 Commando Brigade to counter the armour threat which did not materialise. Nevertheless, its misemployment was perfectly understandable when often it was a question of using everything available to clear the enemy out of his defensive positions. As with the recoilless rockets, Milan is also shortly to receive a more powerful warhead to cope with today's main battle tanks.

Air threat now seen as paramount

After 3 Commando Brigade sailed it became clear to the planners back in Whitehall that it was the air rather than the armour threat which was more serious. Consequently, a week before they sailed, some 5 Brigade battalions were ordered to ditch their Milans and take instead 0.50 Brownings with improvised anti-aircraft mounts. In spite of being very unwieldy to carry, they proved to be a very useful addition, but the decision to take them did reflect the fact that the British Army had nothing in service, and still does not, to supplement small arms and Blowpipe, of which there are never likely to be enough, at battalion level. This is out of step with both Britain's allies and the Warsaw pact, who have self-propelled air defence gun systems, the Soviet ZSU 23-4 and German Gepard being two prime examples. The Royal Ordnance Factories have produced the Centurion-Sabre, mounting twin 30mm cannon on a Centurion tank chassis, in conjunction with the French firm of Thomson-CSF, and Marconi have a similar 30mm system in their Marksman, but these are purely commercial projects and the British Army is unlikely to be able to afford them, in view of what are perceived as more pressing needs, in the foreseeable future. Thus a crucial gap in the air defence layout will remain.

Another cause of more immediate concern was the 81mm mortar. Apart from the fact that the mortars suffered very badly from sinkage in the soft ground, which meant that they had to be constantly recalibrated, there were a number of cases of broken bipods and cracked baseplates, brought about by the intensity of fire which they were required to put down, combined with the fact that they often found themselves positioned on sloping ground. Indeed, at one time during the Battle of Tumbledown, the 2nd Battalion Scots Guards Mortar Platoon had only one mortar working out of six. This was something which had not been noticed during peacetime trials and training and illustrates only too well the fact that there is no better laboratory than battle to test weapon systems.

One final point concerning infantry weapons was the performance of the individual night sights. The troops on the ground generally felt that the Argentinians had very much more effective image

Paras firing an 81mm mortar. It proved difficult to use on the soft, peaty ground in the Falklands with a tendency to get bogged down.

intensification devices. This was mainly because they were smaller and lighter and thus made the rifle less cumbersome to handle when they were fitted. The British were using first generation night sights, but since then a second generation, half the size and more efficient has been produced, and optronics firms have already produced a third generation. It will be this that is likely to be fitted on SA-80, although, at the time of writing, the Ministry of Defence had not yet issued a specification.

The Army's Clansman range of battlefield radios in general worked very well, and the most difficult problem was the resupply of radio batteries. They stood up well to the severe conditions of the Falklands and only the antennae proved vulnerable.

DMS to get the boot

One aspect of equipment which was particularly severely tested was personal clothing, and it proved to be the final death knell of the current Army boot, the Direct Moulded Sole (DMS). Yet, like so many other pieces of equipment used on the Falklands, this was already shortly to be replaced, but its successor was not available in time. The DMS boot took over from the leather soled ammunition boot in the 1960s, with its rubber sole being more flexible than its pre-

decessors. Its main problem is that water seeps in through the lace holes, and in the boggy conditions of the Falklands this led to a universal epidemic of trench foot, although only some forty men, thanks to constant individual attention to feet, had to be evacuated with this complaint. For many soldiers, too, the fact that puttees had to be worn with the boot was an added inconvenience in the time taken to put them on. Most considered the Argentinian high boot very much better, and many units, recognising from the start the disadvantages of the DMS boot, gave their members much latitude in their choice of footwear. As for the new British boot, a forerunner of it is the Northern Ireland patrol boot, higher and considerably lighter than the DMS boot, and designed for urban patrolling. It is not, however, robust enough for operations in rough terrain, and a heavier version is now on general issue. Apart from reaching above the ankle, the tongue is sealed to the inside of the boot, which should prevent water from seeping through the lace holes.

Apart from the boot, the rest of the personal equip-

Modifications: new boot, new lightweight webbing, and the 5.56mm Individual Weapon all mark recent changes in British Army equipment.

ment used on the Falklands — Disruptive Pattern combat suit, quilted inner suit, webbing and sleeping bags — stood up well. This is one area, however, which does not need to be tested in battle, and the British Army has plenty of experience in training in adverse weather conditions. One point to note is that the bergan rucksack proved invaluable. Although on issue to 3 Commando Brigade and the permanent battalions in 5 Brigade, the Scots and Welsh Guards, because they were placed under command of the latter at short notice, did not hold bergans in their stores, and these had to be obtained from civilian sources and hastily dyed. Clearly, the Army will have to hold more stocks in reserve in future. Although the equipment did prove itself once more on the Falklands, there is no room for complacency and the Army's Stores and Clothing Research and Development Establishment (SCRDE) at Christchurch in Hampshire, is continually investigating new materials in order to develop personal clothing and equipment which is both robust and comfortable.

There was only a very limited amount of logistic transport taken to the Falklands, because of lack of space and the few roads and tracks on the Islands. Nevertheless, the Land-Rover and the Swedish Bv202 over-snow tracked vehicle, which British forces use in Norway, both performed satisfactorily.

A final and very important aspect is medical. During the preparations for the recapture of the Islands much stress was laid on a high standard of individual First Aid expertise. So often lives can be saved in battle through immediate attention to casualties, and this was undoubtedly reinforced during the campaign. One particular departure from previous practice was to issue soldiers with saline drip equipment and teach them how to use it, which they did do on occasion. It is thus likely that in the future every soldier, and not just battalion medics, will be equipped with an individual First Aid kit.

Compared with the experience of the Royal Navy and, for that matter, the Royal Air Force, the Falklands 'laboratory' produced few dramatic findings in terms of British Army weapons and equipment. Where shortcomings were identified, modifications were often already in hand, and for the most part the experience confirmed that, like the Army's approach to training, their 'hardware' philosophy is on roughly the right lines within the budgetary restrictions with which the Armed Forces are plagued. The reason for this is not hard to find. For the Navy, and to a lesser extent the RAF, the Falklands was the first war that they had been involved in for many years, and indeed there has been little naval action *per se* throughout the world since 1945. The British Army, on the other hand, has had only one year, 1968, since 1945 when it has not been involved in some form of active service, and hence it has had much hard practical experience on which to build.

EQUIPPING THE RAF: HARRIER IMPROVED

Existence of two major runways on the Falklands obviously takes the pressure off the STOVL Harrier family, which were all Britain had in the way of air-combat aircraft during Operation Corporate; but the Harriers continue to be vital to RAF forward planning, even after they begin to be supplemented by the more capable Harrier GR.5 in 1986–87. One cannot over-emphasise how difficult it is for a service such as the RAF to stick to its principles when it is 'the only one in step'. For financial and political reasons the USAF has steadily denigrated jet-lift STOVL, and even in its colossal ATF (advanced tactical fighter) project, which at a cost of many tens of billions of dollars will lead to a new generation of fighters for use in the 1990s, no interest is shown in the ability to operate away from giant fixed airbases. The only requirement is for the ability to 'take off between the bomb craters', nothing being said about the landing! In such a world, the RAF could fatally easily lose its nerve and give up the precious Harrier altogether.

Fortunately, this is not the case, and instead the problem has been that 60 Harrier GR.5s is hardly going to be enough. This almost completely new-generation Harrier incorporates several design changes compared with the US Marine Corps' AV-8B, several of them the direct result of the Falklands fighting. Most of the fundamental design features have been accepted unchanged by the RAF, and all add to the aircraft's reliability, ease of field maintenance and simplicity of operation. To the pilot the biggest advance will be the flight stability and effortless control, even in the previously very tricky regime during an accelerating or decelerating transition on takeoff or landing. In the GR.3 there is constant side-to-side wander of the nose, lateral stick inputs are needed all the time to hold the wings level and avoid yaw, and the pilot has to concentrate to stay alive. With the GR.5 the basic flight qualities are enhanced and backed up by an improved digital flight control and stability augmentation system which lets the pilot almost sit there and let the aircraft get on with it. A further immediately noticed improvement is that the pilot does not have to hunch over his sight but can sit bolt upright, leaning back comfortably under the giant bulged canopy, with a superb view in all directions yet able to look straight ahead through the wide-field-of-view HUD (head-up display).

The most important updates being made in

RAF Harrier GR.3 with laser designator and armed with 4 SNEB rocket pods. Shortly, these will begin to be replaced by the modified GR.5 version.

existing Harrier GR.3s are those concerned with EW (electronic warfare), and Falklands experience has naturally also read across to the GR.5. Obviously, as the world leader in EW in World War II the RAF had not simply given up interest in the subject, but had been crippled by funding restrictions exerted by the Treasury over many years. Thus, at the start of Operation Corporate not one Harrier, nor one RN Sea Harrier for that matter, had any EW equipment of any kind apart from a simple RWR (radar warning receiver) which gives a broad indication of whether the aircraft is being illuminated by a hostile radar. Nothing had been done to equip either aircraft with an active ECM jammer, or even with a simple chaff/flare dispenser such as are carried by almost all modern aircraft intending to enter defended airspace.

As an immediate stop-gap chaff bundles were jammed between bombs and racks, and under the airbrake, but this embarrassing situation at last released funding for a proper installation. This naturally is a long-term project, but as a more immediate palliative much was done within days to give the Harrier and Sea Harrier at least some electronic protection, and both modifications have since been made standard in all existing squadrons where circumstances are thought to require it. One was a standard off-the-shelf dispenser, the American Tracor ALE-40, a normal installation of which comprises four boxes each containing 30 chaff cartridges or 15 IR flares, plus a chaff/flare programmer and cockpit control unit. ALE-40 has been fitted in various forms, usually as a scab (blister) on the side of the rear fuselage or on the sides of large underwing pylons, on such aircraft as the F-4, F-5, F-16 and even Hunter. As soon as President Reagan gave up his even-handed approach and expressed full support for Britain, a Tracor engineer flew to London with a complete installation plus the manuals. On 4 May 1982 work began at Wittering, putting the dispenser in the rear fuselage attached to a ventral access door. Ten more GR.3s were equipped in short order.

The other installation was home-produced, and it was an impressive achievement in difficult circumstances. It is difficult or impossible to attach available ECM jammer pods to a Harrier, but the MSDS team succeeded in the challenging task of packaging existing jammer hardware into a Harrier gun pod! Apart from having a ventral emitter dome, the resulting pod is aerodynamically and ballistically interchangeable with the standard 30mm Aden pod, so at the small cost (on most missions) of halving the number of guns the GR.3 was given a very effective active ECM jammer. Nose and tail emitter fairings fitted the original pod shape, that at the front covering the gun muzzle aperture. MSDS invented an entirely unofficial code name, Blue Eric, and delivered nine jammer pods by 21 May 1982. Thus, Harriers in the South Atlantic at the close of the conflict had two EW installations that a few weeks earlier had not existed.

One Harrier GR.3 was hastily modified to launch the big AGM-45 Shrike anti-radar missile. Also carried by Vulcans, this 390lb weapon, with a length of 10ft (3.05m), was urgently needed to home on to and knock out Argentine radars based on the Falklands. This installation (on the GR.3) did not see action, but subsequently the RAF recognised that it had to do something urgently to rectify its lack of an anti-radar missile. BAe Dynamics came up with its own weapon, the new-technology Alarm (actually standing for air-launched anti-radiation missile, though the first two letters could better be interpreted as Advanced Lightweight). Much lighter than rival missiles, so that it can be carried in groups of two or three where Shrike or Harm must be carried singly, Alarm won over US opposition in 1983 and is now in production for the RAF (and it can also be carried by the Sea Harrier). It will totally transform the RAF's performance against high-value surface radars, carried by warships as well as on the land, but the GR.3 will have to wait until

Sea Harrier keeps a watchful eye over Soviet aircraft carrier *Kiev* making her way up the Channel. On her deck can be seen two of the Soviety Navy's Forger VTOL aircraft. Only Britain and Russia have Navy VTOLs.

Tornado and Harrier GR.5 squadrons have been equipped with this new missile.

Alarm is a long-term addition to existing Harriers, and so is the Zeus internal EW installation. Almost certainly, without Falklands experience this would never have got past the Treasury, not least because each installation will cost more than the original price of a complete Harrier back at the start of Harrier production! The overall programme, including development and service support, is priced at '£100 million plus'. The prime contractor is MSDS, which will supply a complete integrated system including a replacement RWR linked via a

computer and cockpit controls with an internal multi-mode active RF (radio frequency) jammer produced by Northrop, and with internal chaff/flare dispensers. Installations in RAF Harrier GR.3s, numbering possibly 50 aircraft in all, are to be made by BAe. In late April 1984 it was announced that Zeus will also be fitted to the RAF Harrier GR.5.

Yet another item missing from RAF Harriers at the start of the Falklands war was the 'smart' (laser-guided) bomb. These precision attack weapons had been used in vast numbers in Vietnam and were far from new, and the Ferranti Type 106 laser had been installed in the RAF Harriers (as a retroactive modification for more than half) in order that they should have the capability of locking on to ground targets marked by friendly lasers and also of guiding their own smart weapons. During the closing stages of Operation Corporate Paveway II Mk 13/18 weapons were hurriedly assembled in the field by adding to ordinary 1,000lb bombs the nose and tail guidance needed. Made by Portsmouth Aviation under licence from Texas Instruments, the conversion kits had not previously been available, and had never even been seen by RAF Harrier pilots. Indeed, the kits were dropped from C-130s on an air-refuelled round trip to the Task Force on 27 May 1982!

Today the LGB (laser-guided bomb) is a familiar weapon to many RAF squadrons equipped with the Harrier, Buccaneer, Jaguar and Tornado, the British production being expected soon to switch to the next-generation Paveway III, for which BAe Dynamics supplies Dart high-precision gyros. The Series III weapons have flick-out wings and a micro-processor, and can be dropped from treetop height.

Just as RAF Jaguars replaced by Tornados are being concentrated in one large combat wing based at Coltishall, so are Harriers eventually to be concentrated in one big combat wing at RAF Wittering, the two front-line squadrons at Gutersloh probably being the first to re-equip with the GR.5. The last 25 Harrier GR.3s will still be quite young when this happens, in 1986–87, and studies are continuing to see how far they are worth updating. A Phase 7 rebuild would add a Sea Harrier type nose and comprehensive updates throughout the aircraft, and at one time the concept of the RAF 'Big Wing' Harrier was based on the need to fit the same increased-span wing to the existing GR.3 force. Any complete rebuild along these lines would be at least as expensive as simply buying extra GR.5s, and it is far from clear what the eventual answer will be.

It may not be facetious to suggest that among the many well-known home truths re-learned during the Falklands war was the recognition that infantry with small arms and shoulder-fired SAMs can hit hostile aircraft, and can occasionally bring them down. Moreover, men with small arms sighted by eye are unaffected by expensive on-board EW systems and countermeasures, and there is now a strong body of opinion within NATO that adheres to the view that it is unwise to overfly a heavily defended ground target even in a small, fast, agile jet painted in low-visibility colour. Accordingly there is renewed emphasis on trying to stay out of range by using stand-off missiles, or by toss-bombing (even with conventional weapons, the concept of the toss having been invented in 1956 in order to allow low-flying aircraft to escape the effects of the explosion of their *nuclear* bombs). Put another way, the retarded bomb may very well be on its way out.

This can be extended further to take in anti-runway weapons and dispensers of mines and bomblets for use against armour. Several NATO air forces are busily trying to equip with costly and sophisticated weapons such as the British JP.233

anti-airfield system, the French Beluga and Durandal and the West German MW.1. All demand a direct overflight of the target — an enemy runway or armoured force — at low level. The point was made during the Falklands war that JP.233 would have been far more effective against the Stanley runway than 'iron bombs' dropped from 11,000ft (3350m) by a Vulcan; so it would, but the point must now be made that attrition caused by close-range ground fire is likely in any future war to be significant, and with increasing inflation and resultant reduced numbers of aircraft in the inventory this attribution will assume increasing significance. By 1990 it is doubtful that *any* aircraft will dare fly over any front-line armoured force or any high-value defended target; stand-off weapons will take over totally.

Before leaving the Harrier family of combat aircraft, it is important to note that their inherent basing flexibility has taken many years to be appreciated. Even today virtually every British Harrier is parked either on an apron at a normal airfield, such as Wittering or Gutersloh, or on a costly specially designed ship, such as *Invincible*, *Illustrious* or (soon) *Ark Royal*. BAe has spent almost 20 years trying to get across the message that vectored thrust releases aircraft from normal bases. The future importance of RDFs (rapid-deployment forces) and the repeated lesson that the conflict that actually happens is never the one that was planned may gradually be focusing attention on

unconventional ideas such as BAe's SCADS (ship-borne containerized air-defence system) and Sky-hook. The former is a carefully worked-out scheme for creating complete air-defence systems in a pre-packaged form which, in any sudden emergency, could be bolted on to previously prepared container ships in about 48 hours. A complete SCADS requires 230 standard ISO freight containers, most of them filled with fuel, food, drinking water, accommodation and everything else needed to sustain a warship over a 30-day period (apart from the basic ship and its own fuel). Other containers house power supplies, weapons, aircraft shops and other facilities for deck-level Harriers or Sea Harriers, Sea Kings, Seawolf missiles, radar, Shield decoy launchers and a flight deck with ski jump. The Royal Navy is sticking one toe half-way into the water by studying the prospects of converting one container ship, but only for operating helicopters and certainly not with weapons or other effective war equipment. In the full SCADS the helicopters are used chiefly for AEW, but of course a small-scale installation could eliminate air defence and use merely helicopters tasked in the ASW role. Either way, it is an obvious way of deploying organic and effective extra airpower at sea, or in a distant trouble spot, in a way otherwise impossible.

Below: Sea Harriers 'peeling off'. Right: Skyhook 'Harrier catcher', and visual alignment system for hookup.

Skyhook

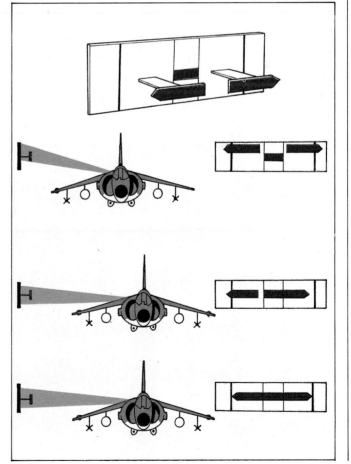

Skyhook is an idea for equipping frigates and destroyers with a computer-controlled hydraulic arm so arranged that, no matter how the ship heaves and rolls, the end of the arm is stabilized in space at the steady forward speed of the ship. Thus a special attachment on the arm can latch on to a hovering Sea Harrier and swing it inboard to the ship. BAe has done enough research to show that the scheme is totally feasible, and it offers the prospect either of deploying Sea Harriers aboard small warships (say, 3,500 tons displacement) in sea states up to 6, which means 99 per cent of the time in most parts of the world, and also of further automating the launch and recovery process so that it becomes totally independent of the local weather. Many armed forces around the world have at last really comprehended the fact that, even if the Royal Navy had possessed all the giant carriers of the US Navy, for much of the time in the South Atlantic in April/June 1982 they would not have been able to operate fixed-wing aircraft. That Sea Harriers and 'landlubber' Harriers were not affected by blizzards and near-zero visibility — such as horizontal visibility of 200ft (90m) — emphasizes the dramatic new possibilities opened up by stopping and then landing, instead of trying to land and then stop! Skyhook takes the concept further and promises to make it totally automated and thus totally reliable, insofar as any mechanical or electronic device can be.

HELICOPTERS: WORKHORSES OF THE WAR

No aircraft worked harder in the South Atlantic than the helicopters of the Royal Navy, Royal Marines, Army and RAF. Some, such as the Wessex and Scout, were of ancient conception and usually were individually old helicopters. The central workhorse, the Sea King, was far from new in basic design but the machines themselves were often quite young. Newest of all were the Royal Navy Lynx and the single RAF Chinook that survived the *Atlantic Conveyor*.

It is well known that the whole fleet of helicopters was flogged mercilessly, combining flying rates from 5 to 15 times normal for peacetime with appalling weather, invariable overloads beyond normal limits and inevitable relaxation of maintenance procedures. This did not apply so much to the Army scouting and liaison machines, but was certainly the case with all the Sea Kings which emerged with flying colours. One ASW squadron (No 826) of nine kept two

aircraft on station guarding the task force continuously for 30 days, each Sea King HAS.5 averaging 160 hours flying during that period. Another unit, 846 Sqn, equipped with the Sea King HC.4, operated its seven helicopters from all kinds of ships and from temporary hides ashore, but, despite winds up to 60 knots and driving rain and ice, lifted 520 armed troops and 1,000,000lb (over 450 tonnes) of stores ashore in a single day.

The newest of the helicopters, the Royal Navy Westland Lynx HAS.2, set an all-time record for intensive utilization overall. No 815 Sqn, deployed aboard various ships, operated throughout the winter blizzard to log 3,042 hours 50 min, in the course of which the number of deck landings reached 4,405.

It takes something like a war in the South Atlantic winter to sort the good from the bad, and drive home various lessons that had been learned in round-table committees years earlier but not acted upon. The classic case was the AEW (airborne early-warning) helicopter, which had consistently been refused funding by the Treasury to save money. It is doubtful

Mk V AEW (Airborne Early Warning) Sea King HAS 5 equipped with Thorn EMI Searchwater radar — fitted and tested in an astonishing 2 weeks.

that there has ever been such a costly saving in recent British military history.

Another lesson was that it is no saving to fail to equip flying machines — fixed-wing as well as helicopters — with the best possible avionics and aids to reduce the pilot work-load. For example to save money no AFCS (automatic flight control system) or all-weather navigation aids were fitted to any of the Army machines involved. Thus the Scouts and Gazelles, which had had to be frantically readied for action at the last minute by adding many items that should have been fitted from the start (such as armour, rocket and flare launchers and IFF trans-ponders), had to be flown manually all the time with hardly any more aids to the pilot than he would have had in World War I! This is not a serious problem over England in summer, but it was no joke when the pilot was surrounded by 60ft (18m) waves on a dark night and ready to drop with fatigue. One last-minute add-on, the radar altimeter which gives a continuous read-out of the distance down to terra firma, is credited with saving many helicopters and many lives.

Right: Army Lynx with prototype Racal Avionics Management System designed to reduce pilot strain. Below: Westland Scout observation helicopter, radar warning receiver on nose.

Like the Marines the Army fly with a single pilot, the man in the left-hand seat being a crew-member detailed to assist with radio, observation, navigation and other chores. It has long been practice to furnish him with basic skills to try and bring the machine home should the pilot be incapacitated, but as a result of South Atlantic experience it is becoming increasingly plain that the RAF and Royal Navy had got it right in using two fully rated pilots sitting side-by-side.

One unexpected feature of the campaign was the way the old Scout AH.1 stood up to the harsh conditions, while the more modern Gazelle failed to do so. The streamlined Gazelle had a good record in peacetime usage, but in the Falklands it suffered severely from various forms of damage and unserviceability. It has been said in jest that future helicopters should do their flight test programme based in South Georgia instead of at the maker's field.

As far as Britian is concerned the main future helicopters are the various new versions of the Lynx and Westland 30, and the Anglo-Italian EH.101. The former have the great advantage of the massive background of Lynx flying, which instead of highlighting deficiencies has merely confirmed the

A Royal Navy Lynx helicopter armed with Sea Skua missiles (which were used in action for the first time in the South Atlantic), with advanced electronics fit visible on nose.

Lynx as the best medium helicopter flying today. In the South Atlantic its comfort, lavish equipment, modern flight deck, automaticity and amazing flight agility caused its crews to be envied. Their missions were not exactly push-overs, but its comprehensive EW (electronic warfare) and IFF systems, all-weather navigation systems and outstanding radar, and modern auto flight-control system meant that even in the most impossible conditions a Lynx could be flown on task in a relaxed manner, with low cockpit workload.

One can include the British Aerospace Sea Skua anti-ship missile along with the Lynx as deserving of praise. This weapon had not been cleared for service in April 1982, but some were sent south with the task force. On the first combat mission with Sea Skuas the Lynx crew had not attended any instructional course and had not even read any weapon-system manuals. They did, in fact, make some mistakes, but that did not stop every Sea Skua fired in that campaign scoring a direct hit.

As for the EH.101, this will unquestionably be an all-can-do helicopter which has already absorbed the fullest lessons of the South Atlantic experience. Originally planned as a Sea King replacement (but now being developed for many combat missions as well as civil airline use), the EH.101 will have composite construction rotor blades, total de-icing throughout and an airframe virtually without fatigue problems. Fatigue, as in humans, has tended to hit the overworked Falklands helicopters in the period after mid-1982, but two Sea Kings — one RAF and one RN — have been fitted with detailed strain-gauges and instrumentation to measure actual inflight stresses and see which cause the most long-term damage.

INDEX

Picture Credits:
Aerospatiale 74B
Alvis Ltd 124
Aviation Photographers International 13, 15, 59T, 62C, 62B, 64
Bernard & Graefe Verlag/Tophoven 49
Blohm & Voss 87B
G L Bound 8/9, 11L&R, 14, 16, 17, 18, 19
British Aerospace 55, 57, 59B, 62T, 116, 118, 133, 136
David Brown Ltd 33L
P Brown (MOD) 108
Martin Cleaver 80/1
COI F/C, 100, 101T&B, 113
M K Dartford 86
Dassault 75T
Editorial Atlantida 74T
Engins Matra 56
Euromissile 123
Express Newspapers 32, 79, 84/5T, 87T
P Graves 70B
Harland & Wolff 115
Hertford Times 40
Hollandse Signal Apparaten 117BR
Howaldts Werke Kiel 35
P King 10/11
Lasergage 126B
Marconi Ltd 121
MARS 117BL
Marshalls of Cambridge 63
McDonnell Douglas 119
MOD (Army) 43, 45, 54/5, 89, 90/1, 104, 123T, 126T, 131
MOD (RN) 2/3, 20/1, 22/3, 31, 33R, 34, 36/7, 39, 47T&B, 65, 70, 81, 82, 83T&B, 120, 134/5
MOD (RAF) 53
NATO 96, 110
Michael O'Leary 73T&B, 75B, 77
Racal Avionics 139T
RTK Marine 42
Rex Features 50/1, 51, 52/3
Royal Marines 97, 98
R Shierma 27, 72
Shorts Bros 127, 128
Soldier Magazine 84/5
Frank Spooner Pictures 25, 28, 67, 68, 71, 122
Thomson CSF 23
UKLF 103
US Department of Defense 68/9
Wallop Industries 117T
Westland 4/5, 138, 139, 140, 141T&B

Illustrations:
Alvis Ltd
Peter Sarson/Tony Bryan
Martin Streetly